Letters

TO MY
Grandchildren

*L*etters
TO MY
Grandchildren

———— ∞ ————

CHARLIE W. SHEDD

SERVANT PUBLICATIONS
ANN ARBOR, MICHIGAN

Vine Books is an imprint of Servant Publications especially designed to serve evangelical
Christians.

Efforts were made to determine and credit the copyright holders of materials quoted in
this book that did not originate with the author. Any omissions of which we are notified
will be corrected in future reprints.

Except where noted otherwise, all Scripture passages are taken from the King James
Version of the Bible.

Published by Servant Publications
P.O. Box 8617
Ann Arbor, Michigan 48107

Cover design: Left Coast Design, Inc., Portland, Oregon

97 98 99 00 10 9 8 7 6 5 4 3 2 1

Printed in the United States of America
ISBN 0-89283-971-6

LIBRARY OF CONGRESS CATALOGING-IN-PUBLICATION DATA

Shedd, Charlie W.
    Letters to my grandchildren / Charlie W. Shedd.
    p. cm.
    ISBN 0-89283-971-6
    1. Christian life. I. Title.
BV4501.2.S4355 1997
248.4—dc21   97-26156
                                        CIP

Contents

About My
Family Editors

Nothing gives me greater joy
than to hear my children
are living by the truth.
3 JOHN 1:4 (New English Bible)

When I began these *Letters to My Grandchildren* I knew at once, "This is much too important an assignment for me alone." So I called together three of my favorite people. Three favorites who all had favorite subjects about our family. Why? Because children and grandchildren should have favorite memories.

* * *

Dr. Peter Shedd's official title is "Professor of Real Estate Law" at the University of Georgia. However, if you were to ask him his number one assignment, he would tell you: "I am the husband of my high school sweetheart. I am also the fortunate father of Jarrett, 11, Anna, 8, and Sarah, 6. Believe me, they are one 'thrill-a-minute trio.'"

Now, since it's all right for fathers to swell with pride, I'll add an item or two Peter would never tell you. Such as, one year recently, Peter was elected (by the students) "Most Popular Professor" in the University Business School. When I asked one of his students,

"Why Peter?" he replied, "It's because he loves us."

Peter is very modest, so I mustn't detail his other honors. Such as being named "Best Professor in the State of Georgia" by one national institution. Sounds like an unusual son and a very proud father, doesn't it? But why not? I have three other fine sons, too: Philip, Paul, and Timothy.

* * *

Dr. Karen Shedd Guarino is "in-house" attorney at Emory University and Emory University Hospital, Atlanta, Georgia: two of our nation's great institutions for learning and healing. Prior to becoming an attorney, Karen was a registered nurse.

Karen is my only daughter, so of course she's extra special. One of my favorite Karen titles is "the little nurse that prays with patients." Did you know that's strictly forbidden in most hospitals? But what would you do if the supervisors and doctors came to you and asked, "Would you please go to room so-and-so and visit my patient there? He needs your prayers." (Interesting item to note: no hospital authority or doctor has ever objected. Not even one small frown. Always, "Thank you, thank you.")

I mustn't forget one other item you'll like to know about Karen. There are seven hundred members in the "American Nurse Lawyer's Association." And early on in that organization, Karen was elected their president. Some daughter, don't you think? But if you were talking with Karen, she'd get you off herself posthaste. And then she'd tell you about her grandchildren, Zachary, 4, and Alexandria Marie, 1. She'd also give you an earful about their mother, Martha Marie, and their father, Darrell. Of course those four are extra special on this grandpa's agenda, too.

* * *

When I began *Letters to My Grandchildren,* I knew right away I would need some very sharp young input. And where better to meet that need than Kristy, my senior granddaughter. A graduate from the University of Georgia, Kristy has recently taken on a new career. From vice president of the Georgia Chamber of Commerce, she has become a traveling salesperson for Tiffany Corporation. Of course, they'll find out soon they're fortunate to have her. SMART, WISE, and BEAUTIFUL, that's Kristy. Plus a super selection as Youth Advisory Editor for our book.

* * *

I'd also like to add a word in the professional arena. There is no way any author could ever find adequate words to thank the wonderful people at Servant Publications:

Heidi Hess, my friend and editor parexcellence.

Bert Ghezzi, vice president and editorial director.

Don Cooper, president and publisher.

Plus the many other nice employees who have blessed me by their careful attention to detail, and for their friendship. My deepest appreciation to you all.

It's time to move on. But first, here's a Bible verse to write on your heart. Some day you'll want it for your own parenting and grandparenting:

"All thy children shall be taught of the Lord."   ISAIAH 54:13

I can't think of a better credo for your fun days ahead, can you?

Charlie W. Shedd

Part One

---- ∞ ----

WHAT ARE YOU LIKE, AND WHAT ARE YOU HOPING FOR?

*I never knew
anyone like me.
Could it be because
the Lord thought
one like me was
enough?*

I will praise thee; for I am fearfully
and wonderfully made: marvelous are
thy works; and that my soul knoweth
right well.

PSALM 139:14

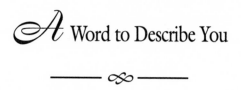

$\mathscr{A}$ Word to Describe You

———— ∞ ————

Dear A to Z:

If you could have only one single word to tell what you are like, what would it be?

Write it here: _____

Love, Grandpa

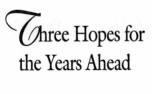 Three Hopes for the Years Ahead

Dear A to Z:

This time you have three choices. Three hopes. So look now to your future and pick one word for each of these questions:

1. What word will I choose to describe my hopes for me when I finish my education?

   One word: _____

2. When I have been at my job long enough to deserve my first promotion, I hope to be:

   One word: _____

3. Dream a little now. You have reached the age of eighty-two. These days your time is limited and you know it. But you are given the choice of one single word for your tombstone.

   One word: _____

Love, Grandpa

As we grow older,

we realize more and

more what Jesus

meant when he said,

"Except ye ... become as little children, ye shall not enter into the kingdom of heaven."

MATTHEW 18:3

Stories from
Grandpa Charlie

———— ∞ ————

Dear A to Z:

It's hard for you to imagine that some day you'll be eighty-two. But I do hope you'll grow that old because eighty-two is a wonderful age. It's particularly wonderful because of all you've learned, and because of all the things you remember.

What a storeroom full of happenings and memories will be yours. Oh sure, there are things you don't like to remember. But here's a piece of grandfatherly advice.

Beginning right now, turn your negatives over to the Lord. Concentrate on the positives. Thank God for them. Deposit them in your memory bank. You'll be glad you did.

Every one of the stories in my letters will contain a truth for you to think about. Over and over the Bible says, "Grow in "wisdom." So as you read on, ask yourself, "How could these words make me a wiser, better person? How do these stories fit me?"

My old wrestling coach would shout at us from the bench: "Keep your head screwed on and your brains turning over." That's good advice for almost anything, isn't it?

So real often, ask yourself, "How does this story fit me? And the little extras along the way, what are they trying to teach me?"

Love, Grandpa

—— ∞ ——

A fool thinks he needs no advice, but a wise man listens to others. PROVERBS 12:15, LB

—— ∞ ——

𝒲hy All My Letters Begin "Dear A to Z"

FROM ALEXANDRIA TO ZACHARY

TWO WONDERFUL GREAT-GRANDCHILDREN

PLUS EIGHT OTHER SPECIALS

Dear A to Z:

Before we go further I should tell you some things you'll need to know: Like why "Dear A to Z"?

"Dear A to Z" will have more meaning if I introduce my grandchildren. First, my two "A" granddaughters, Amanda and Anna. But that's not all the "A's." Meet my brand new great-granddaughter. Her name is "Alexandria," and oh my is she beautiful.

Nice girls, my "A's." But so are Kristy, Martha Marie, Misty, Windy and Sarah. Each and all very beautiful.

But we're not through yet. Two more favorites finish my list of grandchildren. Jarrett*, my only grandson. Then Zachary, my only great-grandson.

So that's the origin of "Dear A to Z" and isn't this a wonderful fact? A to Z takes in every grandchild of every name. Which means all God's children everywhere, doesn't it?

Love, Grandpa

* Jarrett was the child editor of my book, *What Children Tell Me about Angels* … And does he ever know a lot about angels!

Part Two

———— ∞ ————

BE WHAT YOU IS

What lies behind us and what lies before us are tiny matters compared to what lies within us.

The Cowboy's Tombstone

———— ∞ ————

Dear A to Z:

Epitaphs, as you may know, are special sayings on tombstones. You can find them in cemeteries, and reading them makes a fun hobby. Here's one I especially like:

**Be
What You Is
Cuz
If You Be
What You Ain't
Then
You Can't Be
What You Is**

This epitaph came from a friend who said he knew only two things about it.

1. Chances are, it came from way out West.
2. Some western gunslinger must have lost his last fight.

Not much information for something so unusual. But whoever he was, he gives us something to ponder, doesn't he?

Keep your thinker turned on to "Be what you is."

Love, Grandpa

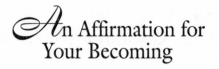

An Affirmation for Your Becoming

Dear A to Z:

Looking back at our "Be What You Is" epitaph, here are some more questions for you:

1. Is you really somebody special?
2. Is you someone with an important purpose?
3. Is you here because you're part of an overall plan?

If your answers are "yes, yes, yes," here's an affirmation for you:

I Am a Special Creation
of My Heavenly Father.
I Am the Only One He Made Like Me.
He Put Me Here Because He Needs Me.
That's Why It Is So Important
for Me
to "Be What I Is."

I wrote this affirmation for myself long, long ago and for me it's a winner. I keep it where I can't help but see it often. I can also say it often since it's written on my mind and in my heart.

I strongly recommend that you write your own credo. A credo of purpose, commitment, and joy. Joy in the Lord who loves you so much he has great plans for you.

Love, Grandpa

You Are a Beautiful Person

———— ∞ ————

Dear A to Z:

His name was Thaddaeus. He carried our trays in a Florida cafeteria, and on his uniform was his name: "Thaddaeus." I had never met anyone named Thaddaeus, so I was curious. Who was this fine looking young man? He looked friendly; would he appreciate some questions? He did.

I asked him if he was a student and he said, "Yes, I'm on a basketball scholarship and I made All-Conference this year." I liked the way he said that. Plain, matter-of-fact, as though I might like to know more.

As he put down our trays, I said, "Thaddaeus, that's a beautiful name."

"Thank you," he said, "my mother gave it to me. I have eight brothers and sisters, and she gave every one of us a different kind of name. Then she gave us a Bible verse to go along with our name. When we were very little she had us memorize our verse so we'd never forget it. My verse is Psalms 139:14. You look it up. You'll like it."

Of course when I got home I looked up Psalms 139:14. I did like it. You will too. It says, "I will praise thee; for I am fearfully and wonderfully made: marvelous are thy works; and that my soul knoweth right well."

I liked Thaddeus' verse so much I began to study it. When I meet up with a special verse, I enjoy reading it in different translations. Why? Because this opens up so many new thoughts. I also like to put various parts of the different translations together. For instance, sit back now and imagine that this is your particular composite verse to live by:

"Isn't it amazing how God put me together in the original? Sometimes I feel it in my heart, and it is beautiful."

Did God mean that, for all of us? I think he did. For you, for me, for all his loved ones everywhere.

A great verse, isn't it? Psalms 139:14. And what a wonderful goal to live by.

Thank you, Thaddaeus.

Love, Grandpa

"Serve the Lord with Gladness"

Dear A to Z:

What are you doing to make yourself a happier person? Are you waiting for others to improve your disposition? Well, don't. Feeling good inside you is your job.

So how can you go about this? We've already looked at one way. That's to accept the fact that you are special. The Lord made you special. He wants you to "Be What You Is."

Way number two is to recognize your positives and improve them daily, weekly, monthly, yearly. You *can* make yourself more interesting to you, and to others. Certainly you'll listen to your parents, study for your teachers, but don't stop there. You can teach yourself. So in this series of letters we'll be thinking about a program to make you a better you.

Let's begin with seven points for your own self-improvement.

1. Three of the nicest things about me are:

_____

_____

_____

2. The last time I did something for somebody else without their asking was _____.

3. At paying compliments to other people (saying something nice to them about themselves) I deserve a grade of _____.

4. The last time I studied something I didn't have to study; read something I didn't have to read; looked up a new word I was curious about; did any form of research to improve my mind; or in any way was my own teacher; that date was _____.

5. Following up on number four, on grading myself for regular self-study, self-research, and healthy curiosity I rate _____.

6. For smiling, laughing, and staying alert to life's humorous side, I rate: Excellent _____ Medium _____ Nowhere near as good as I should be _____.

7. The Bible says that we are to "grow up in the Lord." What does this mean? It means God made us and put us here for a purpose. It also means that he is counting on us to make his world a better place.

   If these things are true, then for trying to "grow up" in him, I believe God would give me a grade of _____.

— ∞ —

Some test, isn't it? And how did you do?

No, you don't need to tell me, or anyone else.

But I hope more and more you will be able to say: "Yes, I'm improving because more and more I truly 'SERVE THE LORD WITH GLADNESS.'"

Love, Grandpa

Part Three

———— ∞ ————

You're Smarter...
But I'm Wiser!

*W*itness how SMART even the youngest have become these days ...

A Sunday school teacher warning her pre-schoolers to dress warm one day told this story:

"I had a little brother who was five years old. One day after Christmas he took his new sled out in the snow without dressing properly. I regret to tell you he caught pneumonia and died."

Silence for ten seconds. Then came a voice from the back of the room: "What became of his sled?"

Sixteen Thousand Is a Lot of Young People

Dear A to Z:

There I was in the convention center, watching from where I sat on the stage. Sixteen thousand high-school students were packed into the hall. They had come for an international youth assembly of their denomination.

Listen: they're finishing up "Sing and Celebrate." (Ever hear sixteen thousand young voices praising the Lord in song?) Awesome. I wish every young person on earth could have heard what I was hearing that night.

I was about to be introduced as their convention speaker. What? A seventy-year-old grandpa, facing this mass of young humanity?

Well, I'm here and they're here so let's go for it. But what shall I say, Lord? As I listened closely, here came that Inner Voice.

"Tell them," the Inner Voice whispered, "tell them how you admire them. Tell them you're awed to be standing here. Why? Because you know they're much smarter than you are. Give it to them straight. They're brilliant, and you admire them, you salute them, you applaud them for their smarts. Tell it like it is. They're far ahead of you in so many ways." This is the message that came in answer to my prayer.

So I did what I was told. I gave these sixteen thousand young people exactly what had come to me from deep inside. Every way I could say it, I said it: "You're so much smarter than I am, there's no comparison. You're amazing. You're wonderful."

And the result? As I went on telling it over again in different words, I could hardly believe this next happening.

Suddenly, as if in a single body, they stood. They clapped, they laughed, they shouted, they slapped each other on the back. They waved at me. They blew me kisses. Then at last they took their seats. And I realized that I still had a speech to give.

But whatever could I say after that? First, I could say what I call a "Javelin Prayer." That's a prayer hurled high, fast, quick, only between the Lord and me. To which prayer the answer came:

"Tell them, Charlie, one more time: Yes, they are smarter than you are. Far smarter. But when you have told them that once more, then you tell them this:

YOU ARE WISER THAN THEY ARE.

Far wiser. Why? Because you've had so much longer here on earth to become wise. A longer time to know yourself. Longer to learn about life and other people. And above all, longer to know your Lord; to understand and appreciate his wisdom.

"That's what you must share with them today, Charlie. And here's your text: Psalms 111:10, 'The fear of the Lord is the beginning of wisdom.'"

So that was my text, and I invited them to make it theirs.
And now, dear grandchildren, I invite you to make it yours.

Love, Grandpa

"But Grandpa, Don't You Know Logarithms?"

———— ∽ ————

Dear A to Z:

Kristy and I were enjoying our "Grandpa and Granddaughter" day out. After our usual lunchtime she asked, "Would you like to see my kindergarten room?" To which there could be only one answer.

Off we went, but this was Saturday, so when we arrived the school was closed. Yet because of its location we could still see her room through a big bay window. Putting our noses to the glass, we had plenty to view. And that's how we got into logarithms.

On the blackboard were what looked like somebody's chicken scratches. "Kristy," I asked, "what are all those things? Is it something for *your* class? Whatever in the world could you learn from anything as weird as this?"

Right here I wish I'd taken a snapshot of her standing there, arms on hips. Plain unhidden pity in her eyes.

"Grandpa," she said with pathos in her voice, "those are *logarithms*. Don't you know logarithms?"

I didn't. But to make it even worse, Dear A to Z, that was twenty-three years ago ... and I *still* don't know logarithms.

See what I mean? You really *are* much smarter than I am.

Love, Grandpa

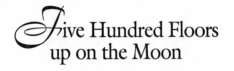

Five Hundred Floors up on the Moon

———— ∞ ————

Dear A to Z:

One night three years ago I watched my grandchildren play games on their family computer. Jarrett was eight, Anna five, and Sarah two.

This was not a toy computer. This was the real thing, and were they having fun. Pure fun. If one button doesn't work, no problem. Punch another, and away the computer hums. I tell you sure, Grandpa was awed.

Me? I started school in a little country schoolhouse in Iowa. Every day I walked with a small black slate under my arm. Chalk and eraser in my pocket. Seventy years gone by, so have a look, country boy; today and far down the years, see the wonders of today and tomorrow.

So let's apply it to your family. When you're eighty-two, what wonders will your children be into? Let's say you call your grandchildren to see what they're doing. Will they live on the moon?

Suppose now you've invited your moon family to the USA for Thanksgiving dinner. Of course, they'll be glad to come. They love you. They love your cooking.

"We probably can't come till Wednesday, Mom. But we can stay all day Thursday. Duncan has a big company event up here on Friday. They've finished the new skyscraper and the official opening is Friday. Duncan's office is on the five hundredth floor and he wouldn't miss it for anything. Of course I wouldn't want him to miss it. He's such a wonderful husband, and oh what a daddy. But, like I said, we can spend all Thanksgiving day with you and Dad. Then we'll fly back Friday morning. We fly our own space ship, you know. Thanks so much, Mom. See you then."

Sounds far out? Well, it isn't. It's far *up*. And if you think it's too far "up," you wait and see.

Remember the slogan is:

Today's fantasies are tomorrow's possibilities.

Love, Grandpa

For I know the plans I have for you, says the Lord. They are plans for good and not for evil, to give you a future and a hope.

JEREMIAH 29:11, LB

"You Ain't Seen Nuttin' Yet"

—— ∞ ——

Dear A to Z:

In a New York taxi cab there was a sign which read:

The past is but prologue to the future.

This particular cab was transporting a businessman to Kennedy Airport. But the passenger, a sophisticated-looking gentleman, was puzzled. Whatever could such a "couthy" sign mean to such an uncouth-looking cabbie? Hair unkempt, clothes unclean, plain scruffy, sophistication zero. Somehow that visor sign and the cabbie's appearance seemed one hundred percent out of sync.

Finally the back seat rider decided he'd ask the driver what such a sign could possibly mean. "Driver," he began, "will you please interpret for me the meaning of your visor motto, 'The past is but prologue to the future'?"

"Why, of course, sir," the driver replied with all dignity. "I will be glad to enlighten you. Dat means, *you ain't seen nuttin' yet.*"

Which is exactly what the Bible says:

> No eye has seen, no ear has heard,
> no mind has conceived
> what God has prepared
> for those who love him.
>
> 1 CORINTHIANS 2:9, NIV

40

Right on, cabbie. If we believe the Good Book, that's exactly how the Lord has it planned. We can count on it:

The past is but prologue to the future.

Love, Grandpa

Three Boys in a Pickup

———— ∞ ————

Dear A to Z:

We were driving that autumn day in the Georgia mountains. The trees were displaying their very best colors. Have you seen the Georgia mountains in their fall glory? If you haven't, put them on your agenda for next year.

Martha would not be here long, the doctors said. But yes, she could probably make the trip if we'd go slowly. So we were going slowly and enjoying it. But the three boys in that pickup behind us were also going slowly. And they weren't enjoying it.

You must not drive fast in the Georgia mountains, and do be careful when you pass. These mountain turns are foolers. Other cars could be coming on before you barely see them. So here we were poking along and here were the three boys hoping. No honking, no shouting, no scary attempts. They had been very patient.

So why didn't I pull over in someone's driveway and let them pass? Plain ordinary thoughtlessness, that's what it was. Of course, I like to think my mind was one hundred percent focused on Martha. But whatever, I was indeed discourteous.

Then suddenly, over a hill, here came a long stretch of road. "You can go now, boys." And they did. But as they passed our car they slowed down for a bit of conversation.

"Something ugly. Pour it on. Give 'em fits."

No. Instead, the boy closest to us leaned out his window. Smiling a big smile, he called, *"Hey dad, it's the long black pedal on the right."* Then as they went around us, all three of them waved a happy wave.

What a class act. We were deeply touched. They could have shouted all kinds of unpleasantries, couldn't they? And I wouldn't have blamed them one bit. It was I, not they, who was being unfair.

What's the message? It's one more hurrah for today's young people. One more evidence of my claim, "You of today's young are not only smarter than we were at your age, you have more class. Sure there are some negatives, some ultra negatives. But oh, you positives!"

Love, Grandpa

Part Four

How to Be
a Blessing to Others

NOTE TO THE WISE:

"I have forgotten your name" is better than "I don't remember you."

$\mathcal{M}$r. Metcalf's Flower Garden

———— ∞ ————

Dear A to Z:

You would have loved Mr. Metcalf. He was a railroad engineer until that awful accident. They were sure he'd never make it, but he did. Yet he was never again strong enough to engineer a train. So they gave him a fancy title: "Superintendent of the Tower."

Sounds high up, doesn't it? And it was, way up. In our little town, Main Street ran across the railroad track. Somebody had to protect the citizens. So there Mr. Metcalf sat, punching buttons to lower the crossing bars. Exciting? Not very. Most of the time he just sat there. After being an engineer, he must have found it boring. But Mr. Metcalf was not one to be bored forever.

Do you know what he did? This perfectly marvelous man planted a perfectly marvelous flower garden at the base of his tower. And perfectly marvelous Mr. Metcalf blessed so many people you couldn't possibly count them.

Groups of every kind … churches, schools, hospitals, homes for senior citizens. He blessed them all. Plus couples and singles holding hands, walking the paths through Mr. Metcalf's flowers. These, too, he blessed. "Everybody welcome. Pick all you want."

Now if you're wondering how there were enough flowers for all, I'll tell you that too:

Most Of The Flowers Mr. Metcalf Planted,
They Were the Kind That
"The More You Pick
The More They Grow."

Hundreds of passengers were blessed by his flowers, too. How do I know? I know because one day Mr. Metcalf showed me a letter the railroad office had forwarded to him.

Dear Railroad Flower People:

Last week we went through your town and because your train stopped for water and fuel, we had such a blessing we could never thank you enough.

When we got off the train, here we were at your beautiful flower garden. What a wonderful display of floral splendor. And all those signs saying, "Help yourself and God bless you." Well, we picked a bouquet and all our way to Montana he blessed us.

You simply could never know what all your flowers meant to us. You see, we were going north to bury our only great-grandson. So little, so wonderful, and now he was gone. We thought you might like to know what a blessing your flowers were. To us they seemed to speak of hope and promise and God really still alive in his world. And oh, how we needed that.

Thank you, thank you, thank you.

There's a lesson for all of us in this letter, isn't there? "Lord, help me to help you by helping others."

And if you keep on living by that prayer, take it from Grandpa, you will be happy forever.

Love, Grandpa

"Everybody Is a Little Bit Lonesome"

Dear A to Z:

Stephanie was the most popular girl in our high school. It had been that way in junior high, too, plus in our church. Whenever there were elections, same song, next verse. How could anyone be elected but Stephanie?

If you had seen Stephanie for the first time, you would have wondered why she was so popular. She was plain, wore thick glasses — a small, thin girl. So how did she do it? That very question is what I asked her one night at a party.

"Stephanie," I began, "you are the most popular girl in high school. The most popular girl at church. Tell me, what *is* your secret?" To which question she blushed, looked at the floor, and said what you would have expected.

"Oh, I'm not either the most popular," etcetera, etcetera. Then when she made as if to leave me, I said, "Stephanie, I'm not going to let you go until you tell me your secret. Please?"

So she settled down and told me.

"Well, I guess if there is any secret, it was something my grandmother said. She and I have always been best friends and you know everyone just loves my grandmother." Yes, I knew that. Everybody did "just love" her grandmother.

Then she went on: "The week before I started junior high my grandmother had a talk with me. She told me her grandmother had told her what she was about to tell me. She said, 'Stephanie, I want you to remember, everybody in junior high; everybody in

49

high school; everybody in the whole wide world; *everybody everywhere is a little bit lonesome.'*"

"Oh. So that's your secret."

"Everybody *is* a little bit lonesome."

They are; and you are *wise* enough to remember Stephanie's secret, too, aren't you?

Love, Grandpa

"But Daddy, I Wanted a Pony I Drew"

———— ∞ ————

Dear A to Z:

One night while I was still an inexperienced father, Philip met me at the door. He was my only child, meaning I knew too little about children. And I was about to find out how much too little.

"Look, Daddy," he said, "I drawed you a picture. Do you like it?" Of course I liked it, and I took him in my lap to tell me all about it. "See this round thing. That's the head. And here are his legs and his tail." Very amateur, of course, with straight lines going out from a not-so-round circle. Very, very primitive.

Then, as his mother called us to supper, I made a colossal mistake. "Philip," I said, "tell you what. After supper I'll draw you a pony."

So off we went together to another super-good meal. (Martha was a great cook.) The three of us laughed and had a good time talking over the day. Our devotions came next, and then it was time for me to display my artistry.

Before telling you what happened I should let you know this: I once took a course in cartoon artistry. So, no problem, I was well prepared for doing a classy pony. And I did. Then, handing my drawing to Philip, I expected a boyish accolade of praise. But no. Instead, saying zero, off Philip went to his room. No further comment.

51

At last it was bedtime and, as usual, he came for our goodnight hug. Carrying both his picture and mine, he handed mine back to me. "Here, Daddy," he said, "it's OK. But *I wanted a pony I drew.*"

Don't we all?

Love, Grandpa

Anna's Teddy Bear Loan

∞

Be ye kind one to another, tenderhearted.
EPHESIANS 4:32

Dear A to Z:

One day when my granddaughter Anna was five, her father and I took a trip together. Peter and I were on our way to see Karen. His sister, my daughter. She was facing a serious operation, and we wanted to be with her.

When we boarded the plane, Peter was carrying a sack of unusual proportions. I wondered what was in it, but I found out soon enough.

Whenever Peter and I get together we discuss all kinds of interesting things. So once again our minds traveled to some heavies. Sports, national happenings, world problems. Plus other simple things like that. Fathers and sons can settle almost anything when nobody is listening. Sounds pretty serious, doesn't it? But don't you worry. We do a lot of laughing, too.

That evening when we were settled down with Karen, we had a great time. Her daughters were there too, and they're an addition to any gathering. So we talked and talked but that's not all. The night before a big operation it's a good idea to laugh some. Keeps us from crying.

At last it was time for our goodnight prayer, so we all quieted down. But right at that moment Peter excused himself. In less than a minute he was back with his odd-shaped bag. And could you guess what was in it? It was Anna's favorite teddy bear.

I wish you could have heard Peter's little speech. "Karen," he said, "here is a gift for you from Anna. This is her favorite night-time friend, and she wants you to have him now."

I could never describe what we all felt right then. First there was a long silence. Then everyone of us smiled through teary eyes. And all of us loved Anna at that moment with a very special love.

So now we had our bedtime prayer together. But right after the "Amen" Peter made another speech. Smiling his special smile, he said:

"By the way, Karen, Anna had an interesting idea. She said she knows her Teddy will make you feel good if you press him against you wherever it hurts the most. But she also said you'll need to get better fast because I have to take him back with me. In other words, he's only a loaner. They sleep together every night and she's sure they'll both be lonesome. So you get better quick, won't you?"

The Bible says, "A little child shall lead them." Our world certainly needs more leaders like Anna, doesn't it?

Love, Grandpa

Blessed is he who has regard for the weak ...
PSALMS 41:1, NIV

$\mathcal{H}$appiness Is Asking Someone: "Please, Can You Help Me?"

——— ∞ ———

Dear A to Z:

The ways of a writer sometimes lead to big cities. Agents, publishers, speaking engagements, media appearances: all of these require big city travel.

As a country boy, big cities made me nervous at first. Chicago, New York, Los Angeles. Masses of people, all strangers, were too much. Noises confused me. I didn't like the hustle. No friends to howdy. Where were the smilers? How could I find a bus, a taxi, and which direction should we go?

Then one day I discovered something about big city people.

Here came a raggedy old man who looked like he'd slept in his clothes. He didn't seem to be in a hurry, like so many New Yorkers. But he did look like a native, and I needed direction fast. So I stopped him and said, "Please, sir, I'm lost. Can you help me?"

He could and he did. Then suddenly his face broke into a beautiful smile and he said, "Thank you so much for asking me to help you, sir. You could never know what that did for me."

Now why would that be? I think I know. I believe it's because the Lord of us all equipped us all this way: He put in me, in you, in everyone, the hidden desire to be a blessing.

Thank you, old man, you taught me something that day.

We bless other people by asking them to bless us.
This is one of our Creator's special gifts of relationship.
And isn't it wonderful?

Love, Grandpa

"Thank You, Reverend, for Your Wonderful Advice"

———— ∞ ————

Dear A to Z:

This was Nebraska, and I was sitting in my study at the church. Just then I heard an unusual knock on my door. It was "unusual" because most people walked right in. We had no receptionist.

Now a young man came in and we shook hands. He sat down immediately and began talking. "Preacher," he said, "I have an awful problem and I need your advice."

Without even introducing himself he began to talk. And he talked and he talked, pouring out his problem. I tell you true, all I ever said were a few mumbling words. Words like, "Oh, I see," "Is that so?" "Yes," "No," and "Hmmm."

On and on he went, unloading his burden piece by piece. Then at last when he'd been here almost an hour he stood up. Reaching across my desk to shake hands, he said, "Reverend, how can I ever thank you for your wonderful advice? You'll never know how much this meant to me."

Then, turning on his heels, he was gone. But this young pastor learned one thing for sure that day: Sometimes people do not need our voice. What they really need is two extra ears. Ours.

Love, Grandpa

Blessing Others Blesses You

Dear A to Z:

Ted Parkinson ran the Ford dealership in our town. He was also a super salesman. All his young men liked to work for Ted because they learned so much from him. "Watch Ted. See how he does it: smooth, honest, thoughtful, caring." Yet sometimes they forgot to apply all he'd taught them.

One day a tacky-looking old man wandered in. Up and down the sales floor he went, eyeing the new cars. But no one approached him. Men dressed like this do not buy new cars. Or do they?

Ted had a rule that everyone gets a welcome in his store. And since his men weren't on the job, Ted walked over, shook hands, and invited Mr. Not-So-Tidy into his office. "Have a seat, friend. Let me pour you a cup of coffee."

And now comes the whammie.

Mr. Scruffy turned out to be super, super rich. Did he buy a new car? No! He bought *five* new cars!

Why?

That very week this old grandpa had been dismissed from the hospital. He'd been there for a long stay, and his doctors had given it to him straight. They could operate, yes, and he needed an operation. Very much he needed it. But at his age, they did not advise it. Too risky. "So we better give you some medicines, wait a while, and see if this helps you improve."

If someone told you that, what would you do? Here's one

thing you'd do for sure: you'd think and make some decisions.

And so did the old buyer of five new cars. Since Christmas was coming soon, he decided *he would give each of his five grand-children a brand-new car.* "Nice kids, every one of them," he said. "They deserve a big surprise."

You get it, don't you? But in case you need something else to help you remember, try this, straight from The Book:

> Be not forgetful to entertain strangers:
> for thereby some
> have entertained angels unawares.   HEBREWS 13:2

Keep those love channels open.

Love, Grandpa

Part Five

——— ∞ ———

LESSONS FROM
UNUSUAL CHARACTERS

$\mathcal{I}$ dreamed death came the other night,
And heaven's gate swung wide.
With kindly grace an angel
Ushered me inside.

And there to my astonishment
Stood folks I'd known on earth.
Some I'd judged and labeled
"Unfit" or "Little Worth."

Indignant words rose to my lips
But never were set free,
For every face showed stunned surprise.
They weren't expecting ME!

A Faith Lesson from the Old Swede

Dear A to Z:

Axel Mandeen was one of my all-time favorite people. A big Swede who came from his homeland because his father thought he should come. Poverty was rampant in their country: no jobs, no future. So Axel came to America.

At the time I knew him, Axel was at the peak of his career. He was the builder of big, big buildings, like skyscrapers. Like some of America's tallest structures. He was big, too, in our church. Everyone loved him with a special kind of love. To be respected for your character, and laughed with for your humor is a sure winner. And that was Axel.

On this particular day he and I were driving across West Texas. We were on our way to a meeting of our church's synod. That means the state body, with an elder and pastor from each church.

It's a scenic drive across West Texas, at least for the first hundred miles. Then it begins to fade into monotony. But it could never be one hundred percent monotony riding with Axel. He almost always came up with different reactions to keep a person thinking. Or laughing. This time it was both.

Nearly halfway to our destination, Axel began to get nervous. We were riding in his car and he suddenly said, "Charlie, look at my gas gauge. I can't believe I forgot gas this morning."

So why not stop and gas up? Answer: Because there were very few filling stations in West Texas. Remember, this was fifty years ago. That meant we might go for miles before we could gas up.

Over and over Axel scolded himself for his negligence, "Vy vould I do dat?... I should be so dumb ... Vots da matter vit me?" Tiresome? Not at first. This man's Swedish brogue could keep you fascinated a long time. But like all repetitions, even the humorous can get boring. So finally I said, "Axel, where's your faith?"

That is an excellent thing to say on some occasions. But even that gets tiring, and I must have said my line once too often. This time he turned to me and gave me a gem I will remember forever.

"*Fait, hell,*" he said. "*Ve need gas.*"

When I was done laughing he began preaching to me. And this was a sermon I wish you could have heard. The theme?

"*Don't you ever blame God for something you should have done yourself.*"

Right on target, Axel. I needed that.

Love, Grandpa

"&yelids Up, Eyelids Down"

———— ∞ ————

Dear A to Z:

My mother was an elocution teacher. She was trained to teach speaking, voice, gestures, facial expression.

> *Now you smile. Now you frown.*
> *Eyelids up. Eyelids down.*
> *Practice. Practice. Practice.*

Then when she had me "Trained to Perfection" (her term), off we would go. Off to the Ladies' Aid.

"The Ladies' Aid"? Who were they? They were the women of our church. Mostly older women, and mostly utterly bored. But why not? One more time the little fat boy (Trained to Perfection and Thoroughly Scrubbed) was about to do it again. Why ever had they chosen his mother to be their program chairman? And for a whole year yet?

The meeting opened with prayer. And then:

"Today, ladies, we are favored with a special presentation. Charles William has prepared another piece for us. Haven't you, Charles?"

Sounds awful, doesn't it? And it was awful. Stories awful, Bible recitations awful, poems awful, mother-written speeches awful.

So if it was awful, why bring it up now? Good question. And the answer is, I know how you feel sometimes. There are occasions when your parents seem horribly insistent, horribly repetitive, horribly "do it, do it, do it, and do it now."

That is exactly how it seemed to the little fat boy speaking at his mother's Ladies' Aid.

Yet sometimes when I'm up there in the pulpit preaching, I think of my mother. And what can I say? Really at times like this there is only one thing to say:

"Thank you, mother. I do owe you a lot. Eyelids up, eyelids down; practice, practice, practice."

So what is the lesson for today? The lesson is that some time in the future you will have this feeling too. You'll look way back down the road you've traveled and say, "Hmmm. Sometimes my parents really *were* wiser than they seemed, weren't they?"

You can count on it, that really will happen.

Love, Grandpa

P.S. Here's a bit of advice on public speaking from my Uncle Edgar: "Stand up. Speak up. Shut up."

The Amazing Mr. Novacheck

---∞---

Dear A to Z:

Novacheck was his last name. His first was Frederick. And he'd come from one of the Baltic countries to our little town. Why here? Because his cousin had come before him, and he'd found work at the mill.

The mill in any Midwestern town is a busy place. Farmers bring their grain to be ground. Grain is stored in tall buildings called elevators. Then the grain can be sold when prices are right. Buyers come. By trucks they come. By horse and wagon, too, and by train. Many, many dollars are exchanged at the elevator mill. This is big, big business.

Some of the mill jobs paid very little. Starting at the bottom, Mr. Novacheck had one of those jobs. Year after year he worked hard. Year after year he saved his money.

Many, many years later, the mill came up for sale. And can you imagine the surprise when Mr. Novacheck bought it? But this kind of surprise was all right with everyone. Why? Because Mr. Novacheck cared about people. He cared enough about the farmers to give them the best price possible. He cared about the buyers. He cared about his workmen. He cared about his town. He cared about his church. He cared about his country.

The result was that everyone cared about Mr. Novacheck. I certainly did, as a young boy, and so did my friends. He taught our Sunday school class, and we loved his stories. He had so many verbal pictures of what it was like to become an American citizen. And did we ever love the parties he and his wife had for us in their house.

Mrs. Novacheck's name was Marika. After all these years, she could barely speak English, but that was all right. Marika spoke with cakes and cookies.

Then one day Mr. Novacheck, growing older than we'd realized, sold the mill. He did keep his bank, plus certain other businesses he'd purchased through the years.

Now comes something almost unbelievable. Clarence died. Clarence was a town fixture with his little black wagon. Three times each week, Clarence cleaned the streets and gutters, making our town tidy. Saying little, smiling, he simply worked with genuine pride. Push the cart, clean the streets, and tidy up for shopping day. And would you believe, Clarence died the very month Mr. Novacheck retired.

Now who do you suppose took over the push cart?

You're right, Mr. Novacheck. Week after week after week, there he was, former mill owner and honorary president of the bank. Push that cart. Clean those streets.

If you were to ask Mr. Novacheck why he would be the successor to a job like this, he would tell you, "why not?"

> *"This is my country.*
> *This is my town.*
> *These are my people.*
> *They have been good to me.*
> *I must be good to them."*

You can see why Mr. Novacheck is one of my all-time favorite people. Fact is, when I get to heaven, he's on my list to look up early. No problem finding him, of course. He's that happy man sweeping the streets.

Love, Grandpa

The Million-Dollar Rain

———— ∞ ————

Dear A to Z:

Lexington, Nebraska is a lively town. We loved it.

We had moved from Colorado to Nebraska and a new church. Beautiful building. Beautiful people. And for me it was like an early heaven.

Farms and farmers, cattle and horses, pigs and sheep, and oh, the chickens. Those farmers' wives seemed to have a thing about feeding chicken to their pastor. Nothing but the best, and lots of it.

Lexington was a fun town, too, especially during "Plum Creek Days." Hundreds came to our town for Plum Creek Days. Rides, contests, horse pulling contests, and lots to eat. Merry-go-rounds, Ferris wheels, parades, cattle judging, and dog shows. Plus whatever you'd like, we'll include that too.

It shouldn't have been called Plum Creek "Days" because it was really only one day. And this year it rained all night, and all the next day. Rain, rain, rain. Not once did it ever let up.

So, what could we do? One thing we could do was have our picnic on the back porch. How many friends can fit on one back porch? Many when it's raining. Here we were then whooping it up, making the best of it.

Now came Ed walking leisurely in the rain. Not at all surprising for Ed. He didn't think like other people, but he certainly did think. Fact is, we sometimes called him "The Wise Old Owl." A leader in the church. Leader in the community. Leader among the cattle men. Everyone's friend. Everybody's helper.

So here he came. "Howdy folks. Great rain, wouldn't you say?" Of course we invited him in, and of course he stopped to "have a word." Ed would always have a hot dog, too, with his words of miscellaneous observation.

"Walk all the way to town, Ed? How many miles is it? Three? You walk it all?"

"Oh, sure. I love to walk in the rain. Why drive when you can walk in the rain?"

This being my first year here, I had been looking forward to "Plum Creek Days" and was not one bit happy about the downpour. "So you like rain, Ed," I grumbled, "but do you have to like it that much today? Look at all the people who came here for Plum Creek Days. Hundreds, and what can they do? Sit in their cars? Turn around and go home? Couldn't you ease it up a little?"

So on and on I went for a while. Then, when I had turned off my flow of woe, Ed smiled his "wisdom smile" and said a line I'd never forget:

"Let me tell you something, preacher. *Anytime you can swap a two-bit carnival for a million-dollar rain you better make the swap and praise the Lord.*"

So now I praise the Lord for million-dollar rains ... and for sage old friends like Ed.

Love, Grandpa

The Wisdom of God
Through George at the Depot

Dear A to Z:

George C. was another of my super-mentors. He ran the depot in our busy Nebraska town. This was back in a different day than yours. Back then, the depot agent punched little buttons to send messages and receive them. They said nobody anywhere could do it faster than George. If you had seen him at his work, you'd agree. This man was extra special.

I was George's pastor. I loved him, he loved me, and I especially loved him because he was extra honest.

This time I went to see him for plain old sympathy. We were having problems with one of our church members. His name was Kal*vin* and you must (a) always emphasize the "*vin*" and (b) never spell Kal*vin* with a "C."

Kal*vin* ran a grocery store and he didn't like anybody who ever worked for him. He was also an officer in the church and that was too bad. Why? Because he was constantly criticizing the Sunday school, the choir, the Ladies' Aid, the men's breakfast club, and the youth program. Nothing was ever right. Including the new preacher, and I was the new preacher.

Right now Kal*vin* was very upset at the new preacher's wife. She had bought some of her groceries across the street. Actually he had even seen her do it.

So now I was visiting George for some of his positive thinking.

He listened, he heard me out, and then he said something I have never forgotten.

"Charlie," he began, "my prediction is that nothing you have done, nothing you will ever do, could be right with Kalvin. So here's my advice for you: turn him over to the Lord. You'll never change him, Charlie. You'll never win him over. So why don't you do this? Every time you see Kalvin, every time you think of him, pray this simple prayer:

"'Lord Jesus, help me to remember you lost one out of twelve. SO, GEORGE SAYS, I'D DO WELL TO *HOLD* ONE OUT OF TWELVE.

"Help me, Lord, to remember that. And please do bless Kalvin. Amen.'"

Love, Grandpa

You Don't Get Nothin' for Nothin' But Nothin'

––––– ∞ –––––

Dear A to Z:

Aletha was one of those wonderful maids you'd like to keep forever. Always busy. Always on time. Always thinking of extra little things to bless you. Like, "I'll take care of the children today. You two go off and have fun."

But that wasn't all of Aletha's positives. She was a great one to come up with gems for thinking through. Like the one that happened up in the children's room.

That particular morning she came to work wearing a bright new blouse. A big one, because Aletha was big. Red, yellow, blue, green, plus other colors too numerous to mention. A sure attention-getter.

Of course, we complimented her flashy look, and she liked that. Most women like that. Especially if they bought their outfit as a bargain.

Every morning she went upstairs first thing to straighten the children's room. Why was that? "Because," she said, "you get that straightened up, every thing else goes easy."

But this morning she suddenly came rushing back downstairs. Laughing, crying, moaning, waving several pieces of her bright new blouse.

"Oh, Aletha! Whatever happened? Are you all right?"

"Yes, praise the Lord, I'm all right. But when I bent over to pick up the toys, that new blouse done split into four different pieces. One for each child, you suppose?" Then, after more of her carrying on and our "We're sorry," she turned philosopher again.

"You know what?" she began, "I bought that thing at a yard sale yesterday for right near nothin'. Oh, my soul, dear Lord, when will I ever learn? *You don't get nothin' for nothin' but nothin'.*"

Yes, you can learn a whole lot from the Lord's unusual people.

Love, Grandpa

The world's stingiest man went Christmas shopping. But everything he saw was "too expensive." Except a fifty-dollar vase, on sale for two dollars. Why so cheap? The handle had been broken off.

"Great," thought the stingy man. "I'll buy this and send it to these friends of mine. I suppose I should send them something. They'll think the handle was broken in shipment."

So, paying the two dollars, he asked the sales clerk to ship the wonderful bargain to his friends. Then, leaving the store, he congratulated himself on his cleverness.

One week after Christmas, he received this note from his friends: "Thank you for the lovely vase. It was so like you. We thought it was particularly nice of you to wrap each piece separately."

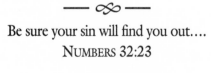

Be sure your sin will find you out....
NUMBERS 32:23

Some More of God's Unusual Characters

---- ∞ ----

Dear A to Z:

God's unusual characters are not all people. Sometimes they're animals. Like Buzz.

Buzz was a champion collie dog. A very proud animal, but why not? He'd won title after title, and he wanted everyone to know he was special. I'm sure you'll think so, too, when you hear what he did to me one afternoon.

We had a big hammock in our back yard. Fastened from two giant trees, it made the perfect spot for my afternoon nap. But almost every day when I went out for my nap, here was Buzz, asleep in my hammock.

So, every afternoon, the same weary ritual. I'd call, whistle, scold to no effect. Even if he wasn't asleep he'd only look at me with no intention to move whatsoever. How could I get him out? Answer: Swing the hammock high and spill him on the ground. Which, of course, Buzz did not take too kindly.

Do dogs really think like we think? I'll tell you a true story about Buzz and then you tell me.

This particular day, sure enough, there he was again, asleep in my hammock. So one more time I swung him high and out he came in a pile. But this time the King of our Kennel decided he'd had enough.

After the customary rude awakening, Buzz waited until he knew I was asleep. Then he ran around behind our garage and began an uproar of prime proportions. Bark, bark, bark. Loud, furious. Of course I woke up, jumped from the hammock, and ran for the scene of all that noise.

Sure enough, there he was, barking his loudest. *Until I arrived.* Then, seeing that he had accomplished his purpose, the champion took off. Where do you think he went?

You're right. Straight for the hammock he dashed. Now jumping in, he looked at me as if to say, "Ha. Ha. Ha. Fooled you this time, didn't I?"

"You sure did, Buzz. What a con man you were. Absolutely nothing unusual going on behind that garage. So you win, Big Boy. Let's make a deal. This really is a huge hammock. Tell you what. You take that end, I'll take this end. OK?" Yes. With Buzz, very OK. From that day on, we lived by our compromise.

Love, Grandpa

$\mathscr{S}$piritual Lessons from the Mules

Dear A to Z:

I do hope that as you grow older, you will become friends with some of God's animal characters. Maybe even some of the big ones.

At the present time, a dear friend and I own together the Georgia State Champion Mule Team. Yes, that's what I said: state champions, and the two biggest mules you ever saw. Kate and Ada. A majestic golden color. Huge, gentle, loving. And oh, how they love to give people rides at church picnics, school picnics, any special celebration.

Now why would I take your time to tell you about mules? The real reason is that all of us can learn so much from mules. *Yes, even some spiritual lessons.*

Spiritual Lesson Number One from the Mules:

A mule will only eat as much as it needs. Then it stops. If a farmer happens to leave the grain-room door open, horses or ponies will rush in and gorge themselves sick. Seriously sick. Maybe even deathly sick. But not a mule.

Mules do like grain every bit as much as horses, oh yes. But a mule is too *WISE* to overeat.

Have you ever heard this little blessing for mealtime?

"Now I sit me down to eat,
I pray the Lord I will not cheat.
If I should reach for cake or bread
Please guide my hand to meat instead."

Sounds like some mule-minded soul wrote that, doesn't it?

Now We Come to Spiritual Lesson Number Two from the Mules:

Let's say the mule is way out in a woody section of the pasture. Here is a mass of old wire someone left behind one day. Now grazing along, a mule or horse walks straight into that wire. And, oh woe, suddenly it is caught in the wire. No way now to work itself loose.

What to do? A horse may thrash around until it has cut itself badly. But not the mule. The mule will stand there patiently, waiting for someone to come.

Sure, there are times when we should work things out ourselves. But then there are times when we need to rely on a power *wiser* than our own.

Do you know how many times our Bible uses the word "wait"? Exactly one hundred times. And many times the phrase admonishes us, "Wait on the Lord."

Now Comes Spiritual Lesson Number Three from the Mules:

When a team of horses runs away from their owner, do you know how that is likely to end? They may run and keep on running. Into a car, into a ditch, into a fence, into a building, into disaster.

Now hear this: When a mule team runs away, off they go. But *they only run a little way.* Fantastic. All of a sudden one of them will say to the other, "This is not the way we should behave. Let's stop this foolishness."

So they stop and look back. "Here comes our master. Let's wait right here." And they do.

I don't need to enlarge on that, do I? So, let's bring this to an end with one simple little prayer.

> *Thank you, Heavenly Father, for your special gifts of nature. And the next time I'm running away, please give me the sudden WISDOM of a mule, to stop and say: "This isn't right. I'm going to wait right here for my Master." Amen.*

Love, Grandpa

Beanie Comes to Church

———— ∞ ————

Dear A to Z:

Our first church after seminary was high in the Colorado Rockies. We had a beautiful view of the mountains from our kitchen window.

But the church was struggling. Struggling so much they had even talked about closing it.

Why had we come here? One reason is that some people like a challenge, and we did. On this day I'm telling you about, we'd been at this church two years and we loved it. It was beginning to grow. People were excited, and we were too. Then came "the wind and the driving rain." I developed throat trouble, and the doctors told me to leave this dry mountain air. My voice was giving out.

In our denomination, when preachers are ready to move, the word gets around. Churches without pastors send their "Pulpit Committee" to listen and decide. How would this one fit us?

One Sunday morning I noticed two strangers sitting near the back door. Good idea, don't you think? "If we don't like it, we can get away fast."

When you realize you're being looked at for a possible position, you know what happens. You try your very best. And I did. But suddenly right at the most crucial point of my message, here she came. Beanie.

Beanie was our prize collie. Beautiful. Huge. And always happy. Right now she was especially happy because she'd found me! Thumping her feet on the floor, thumping her tail on the pews, here she came, totally in charge of the service now.

What would you do? One thing I learned in the ministry was this: *Try to look calm even if you aren't. It will give you time to think.*

So, leaving the pulpit in the middle of my sermon, I gave it my best cool. Kneeling on one knee, I called Beanie to the front. And here she came bounding to see me. Happy. Happy. Then being ever the proper lady, with great dignity she made her way up the steps to join me.

What could I do? What I did was introduce her to the congregation. I told her these were the nicest people ever. Then I told her since she was the nicest dog, they should meet each other.

Turning to them, Beanie barked a greeting. Two greetings. Three. Then she turned toward me, sat down, and offered her paw for a handshake.

Beanie loved what was going on, and so did the people. They clapped, they cheered, they laughed, and some of them even cried. When the fun and laughter had run its course, I turned to Martha. Would she please take Beanie to the kennel and shut her up? Thoroughly?

She did.

Now what could I say to get our service back on its road?

Have you ever said exactly the right thing at exactly the right time? And you didn't know where it came from? Then when you thought about it, you knew. That's how it was for me at this moment. Straight from the Lord:

"Dear friends, I'm glad you were here this morning. You've no doubt heard about preachers going to the dogs. Well, now you can tell your friends you attend a church where the dogs go to the preacher!"

Now the benediction. After that the people clapped and thanked the Lord they hadn't missed this Sunday.

But what would those two strangers say? Would they even bother to "hello" me?

"Hello" they did. Two of the warmest, lovingest, laughingest men we'd ever met. Big time laughs and fun, fun, fun. Plus "Can we lunch together?"

It was a wonderful day for sure. And it led to some wonderful years for us in Nebraska. Yes, Beanie went along. And those two men never got over talking about that church where "the dog went to the preacher."

Now why would I tell you a story like this? For fun? Sure. It still ranks as a number one church service funny for me. But I learned something very important that day. What I learned was:

If you are embarrassed, mortified, thoroughly discombobulated, keep your cool. Look for the funny side, and then pray. Pray one of those javelin prayers. Remember? (Quick, fast, and expect a prompt answer.)

If you will do these things, you will be given exactly the right words for that moment. Words to put you and everyone else at ease. Then you can laugh, and they will. It really is a wonder how the Lord can take what could have been a disaster and turn it into a bunch of fun.

Love, Grandpa

Part Six

———— ∞ ————

HAPPINESS IS
BEING A STUDENT FOREVER

*L*et no man deceive himself. If any man among you seemeth to be wise in this world, let him become a fool, that he may be wise. For the wisdom of this world is foolishness with God.

1 CORINTHIANS 3:18–19

$\mathcal{H}$ow to Be Your Own Teacher

Dear A to Z:

Self-education is not only fun, it's absolutely essential to life's deeper satisfactions. So here's a question for you: Are you limiting your education to what you learn at school?

Don't.

Why? Because school curriculum may only touch the surface. The real school of knowledge is inside you. Higher than the heavens; deeper than the sea; broader than the expanse of any mind, including your mind. Out in the vastness of things to be learned, there are voices calling to you.

So, pay attention to your parents, yes. Pay attention to your teachers, yes. Learn from others out there in your world, yes. But in this letter I'd like to show you something wonderful. *You can be your own teacher, too.*

Let's start with the Bible. Did you know there are some excellent self-help books of biblical knowledge? Go to the library and tell your librarian what you're looking for. Or visit the Christian bookstores and peruse their offerings. Then make your choice and lay out your own program.

You can begin educating yourself in the Bible right now.
How?

Suppose you are twenty years old. Today, you commit yourself to learning one Bible verse every week. But where will you begin?

Begin anywhere—Proverbs, Job, the Psalms, Matthew, Romans, First Corinthians. Or you pick one. Keep it up, week after week, all your life.

Now you are at the prime of life: eighty-two years old. How many Bible verses will you know? Count them.

And what will be happening to you? Your mind will sing with knowledge of the Lord. And your soul will throb with all you know of his glory. Why? Because you are three thousand times WISER than you were when you began.

I know one couple who made this kind of Bible study a covenant between them. What did it do for them? They became the happiest couple I have ever known.

Let's move to another kind of self-education. You could apply this system of learning to almost anything you might choose.

Like humor.

Suppose you decide you'll learn *one good joke per month*. Keep that up for sixty years. You will have close to one thousand laughers in your heart to entertain you. Laughers to share. Laughers to brighten up the world.

And here are some other plus items in this humor education you're giving yourself. One: Almost nobody remembers the old funnies of forty, fifty years ago. You'll hear this question often: Where do you get all these new jokes? Plus item two: Most of the time, your old jokes are far superior to the new ones.

When you're through laughing, move on to more self-education. For example, you can train yourself in your special fields of interest. Like *cooking*. Like *woodworking*. Like *babies*. Like *music.* Like *self-understanding.* And you name a dozen more, or dozens and dozens of your other interests.

Yes, you *can* be your own teacher.

> *"Thank you, thank you, thank you, Lord*
> *that you are so willing*
> *to share your WISDOM with us."*

Love, Grandpa

So teach us to number our days, that we may apply our hearts unto wisdom …. And let the beauty of the Lord our God be upon us.

PSALMS 90:12, 17

$\mathscr{M}$y Favorite Bible Teacher

— ∞ —

Day unto day uttereth speech, and night unto night
showeth knowledge. PSALMS 19:2

Dear A to Z:

My Bible professor in college was everybody's favorite. We
loved this man. Dr. Blake was one of those "student focused"
teachers you'd never forget.

Every year some of his graduates were invited to his home at
Christmas time. And it was always a super event, with super good
things to eat. Mrs. Blake taught home economics in high school.
So there was nothing but the best at her table.

Now it was time for each of us to say a few words. When it
came my turn, I told Dr. Blake how many times I'd wished for
him again. Why? Because, without exception, every student at
seminary agreed. Our young professor of New Testament was
plain awful. In fact, no exception, everybody's happiest moment
of the first year was when we finished New Testament.

Now as I sat down there was a sudden silence. Why? Because
Dr. Blake held up his hand and said, "My dear young scholars ..."
(Another reason we liked him so much. He always called us
"scholars.") "That was an interesting report from Charlie, wasn't
it? But I would warn you all, there is one grave error in what he
and his fellow classmates said. And this is the error:

"Nobody, but nobody, ever finishes the New Testament."

You can see why we liked Dr. Blake, can't you?

Love, Grandpa

O the depth of the riches both of the wisdom and knowledge of God! How unsearchable are his judgments, and his way past finding out.

ROMANS 11:33

Under the Spreading Apathy

—— ∞ ——

Dear A to Z:

On the plains of civilization bleach the bones of countless millions who didn't make it. Weren't they the favored people of God? Why didn't he defend them, lead them to victory, build on them his mighty kingdom of tomorrow?

Search your history book. You will see it for yourself. So many people of power and might wound up in history's stew pot with the dumplings. Why? The Bible says:

"They have forgotten the Lord their God."   JEREMIAH 3:21

Awesome words, aren't they? Early in your education I wish for you a certain happening. One day, something you read stands with arms folded in your path. "Stop," it says, "I will not let you pass until you give me serious attention. I command you to write these words on your heart, not just for now, but forever."

One unknown writer had just such an experience while looking at a history book. The result? He composed this list, which I offer you now for your perusal. ("Perusal" means "super serious consideration.")

Nine Steps in the Rise and Fall of Civilizations

Step 1 = From bondage to spiritual faith.
Step 2 = From spiritual faith to great courage.
Step 3 = From great courage to liberty.
Step 4 = From liberty to abundance.
Step 5 = From abundance to selfishness.
Step 6 = From selfishness to complacency.
Step 7 = From complacency to apathy.
Step 8 = From apathy to dependence.
Step 9 = From dependence to bondage.

Author unknown

Where do you think we are in our own country right now?
And what do you think we (that's you and me) can do to keep us
on steps one to four?

Love, Grandpa

P.S. The Bible says:
"Happy is the nation whose God is the Lord."

PSALMS 33:12, NRSV

Before you speak a word, make it pass through three gates of gold:

"Is it true?"

"Is it needful?"

"Is it kind?"

— AUTHOR UNKNOWN

$\mathcal{G}$od's Beautiful Gift of Words, Words, Words

———— ∞ ————

Dear A to Z:

One of the most exciting free gifts God ever thought up for us is words ... words to contact others ... words to entertain ourselves.

Stop right here: can you think of any greater gift our Creator could give us than "words"?

Words for building skyscrapers or shaping cozy little bungalows ... Words for us to discover ourselves ... Words to share, to lift, to bless ... Words to improve the world.

Words to bring us a smile ... Words to stretch our minds ... Words to cozy up with ... Words for our secrets and Words to share ... Words for someone needing assurance ... Words to make a better impression.

All these for you, grandchildren ... let others be bored but not you ... you can forever be sorting, picking, joining Words ... This is the art supreme ... And above all, remember Words are for you to pray with.

Love, Grandpa

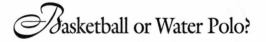Basketball or Water Polo?

Dear A to Z:

Kristy was in ninth grade and she had a problem. So she called me. What a thrill and you'll know what I mean some day. The first time one of your grandchildren phones you for help, you'll see.

The problem for today? "See, Grandpa, I want to go out for basketball. It's one of my very favorite things. But if I go out for basketball, most of the time I'll be sitting on the bench. Freshmen don't make first team in basketball.

"Well, one of my friends said I should try out for water polo. So I've been going over to the pool after school to watch them practice. Grandpa, you know me. I could make that team real easy. Sure it would be kind of fun, but I still want to play basketball. It's like I'm caught in the middle of what I could do now and what I'd like to do if only I could. Can you help me?"

Now for some silent moments between us. Nothing unusual there. Silence to think it through was part of our "help me" visits. Sometimes the best thing a grandpa can do is pray. So that's what I did. I prayed, and here came the answer.

From way down inside me, I thought of an old motto. Very old. It's actually sort of a proverb that has blessed me quite often. A proverb to ponder. A proverb to share.

So I shared it. "Kristy, have you ever heard this old saying? '*A bird in the hand is worth two in the bush.*'"

No, she had never heard it, so there was a long silence for thinking. Then, all of a sudden, she said, "Oh, I get it. Thanks, Grandpa. Thanks heaps."

Do you get it? I hope you do, because it actually fits right into our "Be What You Is" theme, doesn't it?

Love, Grandpa

Part Seven

——— ∞ ———

FORGIVING, FORGETTING, AND STARTING OVER

*T*he Lord is compassionate and gracious,
slow to anger, abounding in love....

He does not treat us as our sins deserve
or repay us according to our iniquities....

As far as the east is from the west,
so far has he removed our transgressions
from us.

PSALMS 103:8-12, NIV

"Me 'n Ronnie. We Got Good Forgetters"

———— ∞ ————

Dear A to Z:

That evening, Philip came storming into the house, mad. You're right. "Angry" is the word. But this boy was "mad, mad, mad."

Of course, it was Ronnie's fault again. Ronnie lived across the street and he was Philip's buddy. But, no sir, not this time. Whatever he'd done, Ronnie could never come in our house again. Never. Never.

So we ate our meal somewhat subdued that night. Somewhat sad. We liked Ronnie. Fact is, we loved him.

Then suddenly, the doorbell rang. Philip, as usual, ran to answer and here he came ... with whom? You guessed it.

"Hey, Mom, can Ronnie have some ice cream too?"

"Of course, he can. But Philip, what about all those things you were saying? Didn't you mean them?"

"Oh, sure," came the answer, "I meant them. But me 'n Ronnie, we got good forgetters.'"

Wouldn't it be wonderful if every one of us could say that? And mean it?

Love, Grandpa

Lord, how often shall my brother sin against me, and I forgive him? Till seven times? Jesus saith unto him, I say not unto thee, until seven times: but until seventy times seven.

Matthew 18:21-22

How Much Would I Be Willing to Forgive?

Dear A to Z (and for all of us who ever did anything wrong):

It was a dark and rainy night in Commerce, Georgia. A cold rain; and dark, dark. But there was a beautiful light in the church. Is there any light more beautiful than the light of forgiveness?

Don and Dawn had called me several months ago. Would I marry them ... again? This is their story.

Don and Dawn had been married thirty-five years ago. The place? Memorial Drive Presbyterian Church in Houston, Texas. The pastor then? It was your grandpa. That was January 26, 1961, and they had done well together after their marriage. They both had successful careers in education. Leaders in their community. Leaders at their work. Leaders in their church. Plus two beautiful children.

Then the unthinkable happened. Don met someone else, someone he wanted more than Dawn. So they divorced.

Was the new marriage happy? Not for long. So he divorced again and headed into fifteen lonesome years. What a giant mistake he'd made.

Now it is January 26, 1996. This was the dark and rainy night. But I'll say it again: warm and beautiful inside the church at Commerce.

Think what it must have taken for Dawn to say, "I forgive you, Don." Think what it must have taken for Don to forgive himself.

But that's what they did. Dawn forgave Don, and Don forgave himself. Unbelievably beautiful.

Now from Dawn: "We had forgotten how important praying together is in love at its best. So we began praying in duet again."

From Don: "She is so right. In every way we needed to get back where we'd come from. That's when we started looking for Charlie."

In my sixty years of ministry, I have never seen anything like this. Love and mercy at its majestic best.

Now, down the aisle they came, at precisely eight o'clock. The exact same date, same time as the original wedding, thirty-five years before. After the ceremony came the wedding party. Members of the church braved an ugly downpour to celebrate. It was a never-to-be-forgotten wedding reception. Refreshments galore, love and laughter galore. Celebrate. Celebrate. Celebrate love at its forgiving best.

Question: any time, all the time, any day, any year, "Am I willing to forgive? Willing to forgive others? Willing to forgive myself?"

I wish you could have been there.

Love, Grandpa

Peter and the Boxer's Swinging Door

Dear A to Z:

Peter was one of the nicest little boys you could imagine. Everyone in the neighborhood loved Peter, especially the Goodes. Ben and Gene Goode were a wonderful couple. They didn't have children, so they called ours their very own. And that was all right with us. Sometimes very all right.

Peter had two little playmates who were extra-special friends. Of course they wouldn't do anything negative on purpose. But then again, maybe. And the story I am about to tell you was one of those "maybe" times.

Ben and Gene raised Boxer dogs. Big, beautiful, the very best. Fine show animals. Super dispositions. The kind that loved to play with children.

The Goodes' backyard was fenced, so the dogs could run freely. But these were considerably more than yard dogs. They were house dogs of the trustable kind. Just one problem. Constantly opening the kitchen door to let them in was a nuisance. So Ben, who was a clever woodworker, decided to do something about this. He built a swinging door in the kitchen wall. Now "come and go, dogs, as you like."

One summer the Goodes decided they would vacation in California. They'd be gone for at least three weeks. But the Goodes were so busy getting ready for vacation, they forgot one important thing. When Ben had made the swinging door, he also put a latch on the inside. Whenever they wanted privacy, or if they were gone, they would take the dogs to a kennel and lock that door.

This time, the Goodes forgot to latch the door before they left. Which wouldn't have mattered much really, except for one thing. Ben had built a beautiful low table for their living room. A table for magazines, books, and one other thing—a candy dish. Always filled. Always the best candy, which the dogs had been trained never to touch.

Let's say you are a small child. Small enough to go through the Boxers' swinging door. You know, because you've done it. One day when the Goodes were home, you tried it. How they had laughed!

Now, just think. If they forgot to latch that door, might they have forgotten to put the candy away? "Come on, guys. Let's give it a try."

So they did, and behold, almost a full dish of forgotten candy. "Think, fellows. Won't this candy spoil before our wandering friends come home? That wouldn't be nice, would it? Of course not, and nobody would ever know. How could they?"

You remember, don't you, I told you Peter was someone extra nice. And so were his two buddies of the highest quality. But something was bothering Peter. Not always, but now and then he wasn't himself. Was he sick? Oh, Lord, please not sick. Yet this went on for weeks and weeks, then months. And suddenly he was all right again.

Why? You guessed it. We didn't know about it, of course, until after Ben and Gene told us. But one day Peter came knocking at their door. And this was their story.

"Peter hadn't been to see us for a long time. You know that wasn't like him and we wondered if he was sick. So, of course, we welcomed him. 'Come in, come in, Peter, it's so good to see you. Let's sit right here in the living room and hug. Have some candy. Oh sure, have some. No candy? Whatever is the matter with you, Peter? You don't like candy anymore?'"

Then, they said, "Peter began to cry. So we let him cry. Then, when he settled down, he did a beautiful thing. He took our hands and confessed. While we were gone, he said, he and his buddies had come in by the dog door. Yes, they had taken all the candy and could we ever forgive him?"

Could they? What do you think?

Love, Grandpa

— ∞ —

"Be ye kind one to another,
tenderhearted, forgiving one another."

EPHESIANS 4:32

— ∞ —

When It's Hard to Forgive Yourself

Dear A to Z:

The little town where I grew up was in a beautiful setting. Soft, rolling hills, majestic trees, lovely homes. The Log Cabin Grocery was our only business, so school events always drew a crowd.

Our school went only from first to eighth grade. For high school we'd go to a nearby city. That was one reason why seventh and eighth grade events were "Standing Room Only."

Now came the night for our junior high play. Packed house again. Excitement high, and I had the lead part. Lucky me. But no, I don't remember it that way. Actually it's still one of the worst memories of my eighty-two years. And I had nobody to blame but me.

I almost hate to tell you what happened, but I think I should. Why? Because I would never ever want anything like this to happen in your life.

Like I said, I had the lead part and I was on stage most of the time. It was never hard for me to learn lines, at least enough to get by. And I loved lead parts.

But this spring season there were all kinds of long-distance swimming races on our river. That was another of my specialties, and every night after play practice I'd head for the river. Then Catfish Reid, my swimming coach, would say, "Ya gotta practice, Charlie. Gotta practice." And I did practice swimming, too.

Practiced too much for anyone who had the lead in our junior high play.

Result? I didn't know my stage lines as well as I should. Because our drama coach was an ace, I got by. She knew me from previous plays. She knew I could ad-lib if I forgot for a moment. Then, if I was a bit fuzzy I'd move toward the curtain. I'd give it a push and, hiding behind the curtain, she'd clue me in. So, back on track, not one single soul would notice. You can believe I loved that lady.

But now I must tell you about Herbert. Herbert was a little country boy. Such a nice little boy who lived north of town. He was in the cast of our play, too, but he had only one line. Just one. Yet for him that one line was every bit as important as all mine put together. Plus, the night of the play, every one of his relatives attended. A big bunch of them came in a group, waiting for Herbert's entry. But it never happened.

Why? *Because Charlie had left out one half of one page, and you guessed it. The half page I left out was where Herbert should have come on stage.*

Herbert was crushed. His big family was crushed. I was crushed. I still feel that way sometimes as I muse on that ugly memory. There's Herbert, standing in the dressing room, looking at me. Plus all his relatives, looking at me as they go out.

Of course, I told Herbert how sorry I was. Many times I told him. Yes, I went to see his relatives and apologized to them, too. But what could I say?

Why do I tell you a story like this? It's so unpleasant. Yes. I know God has forgiven me. But here comes Herbert again, down the road of my memory, and look what I did to him. Plain selfishness, that's what I did to him. Utter carelessness.

Honest, if I could I'd give Herbert every ribbon I ever won in the river races. But I can't, for two reasons. First, Herbert went to heaven long ago. Second, I don't have a single one of the ribbons I ever won in the river races. I threw them all in the river.

So ask it again. Why *do* I tell you this?

Answer one: Because I want you to believe that all God's children everywhere are linked in a network of love. And we have a responsibility to bless who we can, when we can, where we can.

Answer two: I hope you'll be able to build up a strong belief in heaven. Why? Because I'd like so much for you to understand all that heaven means. And one thing you too may need some day is what I call: "The heavenly making up for the wrongs we've done to others."

See you in heaven, Herbert.

Love, Grandpa

$\mathcal{L}$ove Never Gives Up

———— ∞ ————

Ed and Jim lived on adjoining farms. They were best friends, which was a bit unusual. Farmers living side by side or back to back aren't always best friends.

Broken down fences, straying animals, boundary disputes: these do not often make best friends. But after thirty years, Ed and Jim were still thirty-times-over best friends.

At least once each week they'd meet at their adjoining back fence. They'd even had a gate installed there so they could "Put a foot up"—a farmer's term for talk, talk, talk.

Now here comes a sad story. Ed had a son named Bobby. Bobby was one of those boys who could break a father's heart, and Bobby did. A super athlete when he was sober. But day after day, he drank himself drunk. He was often in trouble with the law. This time, big trouble.

Bobby was sentenced to ten years in the penitentiary.

Now Ed had come from the courtroom. He'd called Jim to meet him at the back fence, and this was their conversation.

"Just how much can a man stand, Jim? You know how many times I've set Bobby up to farm, to go into business. And you know how many times he's gone through everything. What would you do if he was your boy, Jim?"

Long silence now. Jim was a kind man who wanted to say the right thing. But he was also honest and he would never be anything else with his best friend. So this is what he finally said: "I guess, Ed, if he was my boy I'd disown him."

I'm glad he said that. Why? Because Ed's remark to Jim will forever be one of my all time favorite pictures of God.

"Jim, if he was your boy I'd disown him too."

Straight from the Bible now:

Never will I leave you; never will I forsake you.

HEBREWS 13:5, NIV

Love, Grandpa

Part Eight

———— ∞ ————

SOME IMPORTANT "DON'TS"
TO REMEMBER

*L*ittle foxes spoil the vines....

SONG OF SOLOMON 2:15

What's All This about Foxes and Vines?

Dear A to Z:

There is no more fascinating book published than your Bible. I hope you attend a church where your preacher makes the Word of God interesting. And here's an example.

In Solomon's time grapes and other small fruit were big time. People from every level of life enjoyed their juices. But the fruit had enemies. Sometimes small rodents came in under fences to destroy a good crop. And one of the major four-footed stealers was the fox. Especially the little fox that could slip under the smallest openings. So that's why Solomon used the fox to make his point.

We're beginning now a series of letters on some of our own little foxes. Little fox habits, little decisions, little excuses unnoticed at first. So many little things can be super dangerous.

You'll think about this, won't you? It's *smart* to realize that temptation is everywhere around us. But it's *wise* to face this question for ourselves: "Am I letting those little foxes endanger the better me?"

Love, Grandpa

$\mathcal{D}$on't Try to Fix Everything

Dear A to Z:

Uncle Edgar was my favorite uncle. He was a school superintendent, and we went to see him often. Aunt Libbie taught in Uncle Edgar's school, and I was glad she didn't teach me. Aunt Libbie was a perfectionist. Do it now. Do it right. No excuses.

This day, as we drove into his driveway, Uncle Edgar was fixing his garden gate.

"Watcha doing, Uncle Edgar?"

"Well, Sonny," he answered, "if we have time after dinner I'll recite you an old list I want you to learn. And I can tell you right now that if you'll remember this one it might save you a lot of work and worry."

You can imagine I could hardly wait until after dinner. Uncle Edgar knew so many interesting things. Useful things: and he knew them all by heart. So now it was after dinner and, just like he promised, the lesson began:

Five Kinds of Broken Things

First: There's the kind that when they're broken nobody can fix.

Second: There's the kind that when they're broken will fix themselves if we leave them alone.

Third: There's the kind that when they're broken someone else has to fix.

Fourth:	There's the kind that when they're broken only God can fix.
Fifth:	There's the kind that when they're broken we've got to fix.

"That last is what I was doing today," he added. "I was fixing *my* gate." But before we started on something else he made me say all five of them back until I could repeat them by heart.

That was so like Uncle Edgar, too, the wise old teacher. And finally, when he knew I could repeat his list, he added: "Five kinds of broken things, and I hope you got the big news. The big news is that the Good Lord doesn't expect any one of us to neaten up the whole world all by ourselves."

Now that really is good news, isn't it?

Love, Grandpa

Some things flow in the stream of your life forever.
With these, you'd better make friends.
Or, if you can't make friends,
You'd better ask the Lord to handle them for you.

Don't Put Off Until It's Too Late

Dear A to Z:

Mrs. Murrow was my fifth grade teacher. I thought she was some kind of monster when I sat under her eagle eye.

She insisted on a high level of performance, especially in English. She gave me assignments which I thought were way too advanced for poor me. But she kept at it with never a let up. You can believe, when school was out that year, it was rah, rah, rah. No more Mrs. Murrow.

But one day when I had grown to adulthood I suddenly realized something interesting. At this moment I was doing exactly what Mrs. Murrow had taught me. Same gathering of materials. Same preparation. Same product. In other words, this lady had really blessed me. Thank you, Mrs. Murrow.

Next I did exactly what you would have done. I decided to write her a thank you letter. So I did. But now run for your Kleenex while I rally my courage to confess. Two weeks after I sent my letter here came word from Mrs. Murrow's daughter:

> Dear Dr. Shedd:
>
> Thank you for writing my mother. I regret to report that she died last year at the age of eighty-three. She often talked about you, and she was so proud of your writing. I'm sure she would have been glad to know that she helped you.
>
> Sincerely, Louise

How do you think I felt when I read those words? Hmmmm.
Just like the Bible says:

> Withhold not good from them to whom it is due,
> when it is in the power of thine hand to do it.
>
> PROVERBS 3:27

And do it *now*, Charlie. *Now.*

Love, Grandpa

'Tis better to buy a small bouquet
And give to your friends this very day
Than a bushel of roses, white and red,
To lay on their coffins after they're dead.

$\mathscr{D}$on't Go So Fast
You Miss the Fun Things

Dear A to Z:

Philip, Karen, Paul, Peter, and Timothy made a lively family. Five children would, wouldn't they? But I didn't worry too much. Our five had absolutely the greatest mother in the whole wide world.

I was gone from home quite often on speaking engagements. That was too bad in one way — I missed so much of the fun. But to make up for it we developed this plan: "If at all possible, Daddy takes one of the children along on his trips."

This time it was Karen's turn. We were riding together way out in west Kansas. As we drove along we saw this sign over and over:

"Stop in our town. See the World's Deepest Well!"

Sometimes the sign pictured a child or two peering down a deep, dark hole.

With each sign, Karen would say, "Daddy, please can we stop to see the World's Deepest Well?"

But I was headed for a high school graduation in a town further on. So I would answer, "I'm sorry, Karen. But we simply don't have time today. Gotta hurry. We'll be lucky to make it."

So we didn't stop and after several more "please Daddy's," Karen gave up. Then as we approached our destination she said something I would remember forever. "Daddy," she said, "I feel sorry for you. You go so fast you miss too many fun things."

Sad story, isn't it? But I'm still grateful for the lesson you taught me, Karen. And ever since that I've tried not to miss so many fun things.

Two WISE words to keep handy when we need them: "SLOW DOWN!"

Love, Grandpa

How beautiful it is to do nothing
and then to rest afterward.
OLD SPANISH PROVERB

Don't Always Settle for the Easiest Way

∞

Dear A to Z:

"Pop" Varner was school superintendent in the tiny town of Diagonal. He also drove the bus part-time, and coached basketball. Because he knew the game and how to teach it, his boys won their league title with boring regularity. But the home town folks thought it was great.

Then one year Diagonal played their way to the State Finals. Sixteen of Iowa's best teams came from every kind of school. In those days the small schools competed with the big schools. So naturally Pop's boys got beat. But Pop noticed something he thought was important.

The Diagonal boys seemed to play better against the big schools. They were classier, sharper, more determined. And Pop liked what he saw. So what do you think he did?

The next year he booked some big city teams far out of Diagonal's class. Naturally, the town people didn't like their team coming home trounced. But Pop kept at it, and the next year they even whipped some of the big schools. That gave the local fans something to brag about.

Then in their fourth season of this heavy competition, Diagonal battled its way to the State Finals. You would have enjoyed watching that year. Pop sat calmly, legs crossed, a twinkle in his eye. And as he watched, his boys defeated Iowa's largest school for the state championship.

Next morning, the state newspaper splashed this headline across its front page: "Little David Slays Goliath Again."

The pensive prophet Jeremiah sums it up like this: "If thou hast run with the footmen, and they have wearied thee, then how canst thou contend with the horses?" (Jeremiah 12:5).

What is the meaning of both the Diagonal story and this unusual verse from the Old Testament? Couldn't it be that "take it easy" is not always the way to long-range achievement?

Love, Grandpa

Thought for today:
"Fast is not always quickest,
and big is not always better."

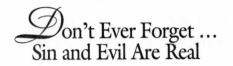

Don't Ever Forget ...
Sin and Evil Are Real

Dear A to Z:

My Martha loved her Bible. She read it often, especially the new translations. And as she read, she wrote notes to herself. Plus she also underlined certain passages that had a special meaning for her.

I invite you now to read and ponder one section she marked for emphasis. And this is the passage I pass along as we think about citizenship. It is a quote from Psalm 55 (NIV), which includes just the words she had underlined. These are the verses she selected:

> "I see violence and strife in the city. Day and night they prowl about ... malice and abuse are within ... Destructive forces are at work in the city; threats and lies never leave its streets....
>
> "My companion attacks his friends; he violates his covenant. His speech is smooth as butter, yet war is in his heart; his words are more soothing than oil, yet they are drawn swords.
>
> "Cast your cares on the Lord and he will sustain you.... But you, O God, will bring down the wicked ... as for me, I trust [the Lord]."

A most unusual passage for special attention, don't you think? Martha was a lover, a hoper, a believer in the quality of human nature. But here she was, deep in some very dark facts of life. So she had marked the warnings for her special attention. And isn't this exactly what we should all be doing?

Life is not all butterflies and roses, is it? "Violence and strife in the city" are a real part of life for all nations, all people.

So what can we do about this? I challenge you right now to open your own Bible and meditate on Psalm 55. Then read it in another translation, or several. And after you've done that, ask yourself: "What *can* I contribute to the awesome fact that 'destructive forces are at work in my town'?"

You will be interested to know that Martha had written some other words I need. Her own words. I'm sure you too will want to add these to the warning written on your heart:

> *"Didn't Jesus make it plain that we are to love all? Yes. But he never once said we are to trust all. Lord, help me to remember this."*

Love, Grandpa

For years in Houston, Texas I had a radio program called, "60 Second Devotional." One morning I quoted someone who said there are 726 known sins.

Would you believe, I had phone calls, letters, and cards asking if they could get the list?

One man was bold enough to include this note in his letter. "You see, Reverend, I'm wondering if I've missed something."

Part Nine

———— ∞ ————

SOMETIMES THE ONLY
ANSWER IS "NO"

*O*ne of those familiar telephone salesmen was up to his usual high-pressure pitch.

"Hello," answered a small boy.

"Let me speak to your mother or father," the salesman replied brusquely.

"My mother is upstairs taking a nap."

"Is there anyone else at home?"

"Yes, my sister."

"Well, put her on."

A long silence ensued, and finally the boy's voice again. "I'm sorry, mister. I can't lift her out of the playpen."

Out of the mouth of babes ... hast thou ordained strength....

PSALMS 8:2

This Year He Would Not Deliver the Liquor

Dear A to Z:

It was so like Bob Jung. When he had the feeling something wasn't right, you couldn't make him do it.

Bob and I were both at the same Iowa college on football scholarships. And Bob was one of our best linemen. I should know. We played side by side in the line.

Do you believe in angels? I do. I've seen so many unusual happenings in the lives of so many people. Like this one:

I had become the first pastor of a growing new church in Houston, Texas.

When you're beginning something new for the Lord, you start knocking on doors. Now here comes the unusual.

One late afternoon I knocked on the door of a nice suburban home. And who should come to the door but my ex-football buddy. Bob Jung and his family had just moved here for a new job.

You can imagine what happened from there. Here we were together again. Only this time, two wonderful wives, both super-good cooks. Two sets of children for playing together. Two minds filled with countless memories from the football field.

Unbelievable: "the brush of an angel's wing."* You can see why Bob and I both believed in angels.

Now to a well-known oil equipment company. Bob is one of their coming young "executives-to-be," a special job for a special person.

This company, like many, remembered their customers with a special holiday gift. They would give a case of the best liquor to their best clients. And, of course, they chose the best of their personable young men to make the deliveries. That was Bob. Personality plus.

But then came the year when Bob said, "No. This year I will not deliver the liquor. I know too many of our customers who already drink too much. Too much for their marriages. Too much for their families. Too much for their own future. This year I was elected an elder in my church, and some of my ideas have changed. One of these changes is for me to say, 'No' when I should say 'No.'"

"Gross insubordination." That's what his boss said. "I can't fire you, Bob. But I can call the president and he'll fire you. You do know that, don't you?" Yes, Bob knew that. But being Bob, he stuck to his decision.

Of course, Bob came to the church on his way home that night. And we prayed. And we talked. And we both knew he might lose his job.

---

*Editor's note: Do you like to read about divinely orchestrated "coincidences"? You might enjoy Dr. Shedd's bestselling *Brush of an Angel's Wing*. For ordering information, look at the last page of this book.

The next morning, here was a special delivery on Bob's desk. The company president wanted to see him. Today.

"Bob," the president began, "I guess you know you could be discharged for insubordination. Ours is a company where authority is to be respected. And I have had a full report on you."

A long silence. Then, the president begins again: "Bob Jung, I called you up here to tell you that this company needs men like you. Yes, I could have told you this by letter or by phone. But I wanted to thank you personally for what you've taught us. All of us. You'll do us a lot of good, Bob. We'll be counting on you."

A thrilling story, isn't it? And I wish it had a happy ending, but it doesn't. As time went by, Bob did become a bulwark in his company.

"But then came the wind and a driving rain, and life was never the same again."

Bob had a stroke. Then two strokes, and more. Why?

Why do bad things happen to good people? Won't it be great when we get to heaven and have some answers? Yes, that will be great. And it will also be great for wives like Dorothy. How do they do it? Year after year Dorothy stood by his bed and cared for him; prayed for him; loved him.

Then Bob went to heaven, and at his funeral it was standing room only. Folks from the church, yes. But company folks, too. All here to pay their respects. Genuine respect.

How genuine? After the service, as I made my way from pulpit to dining room, someone called my name. Turning, I saw five men standing together, apparently waiting for me.

So I went to meet them. One very old gentleman, seemingly

the leader, began with, "Doctor, I want to thank you for that story you told about Bob. You see, I'm the one who saved Bob's job, and it's the best thing any president ever did. You know, don't you, stories like Bob's go on and on until they become legend in a company. A positive legend we can be thankful for."

That was what the man said.

Gives us something to aim for, doesn't it?

Love, Grandpa

— ∞ —

Remember:
"If you want to rise to the heights,
stay on the level."

— ∞ —

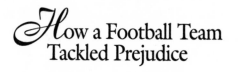

How a Football Team Tackled Prejudice

---∽∞---

Dear A to Z:

Our school had just won the conference title. It was a real thriller. With seconds to play, Eddy caught a pass and made his third touchdown.

For the first time ever, we were "League Champs." Ours was a small college, and almost always we were the underdogs. But not this time.

So here we sat, waiting for the big steaks. Then suddenly a turn of events, and we could hardly believe what we were hearing. This was the restaurant manager telling our coach, "Mister, this is the South, and we don't feed colored in here. We'll feed him in the kitchen, but not here."

How would you have reacted to that? Remember now, this was many years ago, and Eddy was our only black player. Eddy was a freshman, but in spite of that he'd made all-conference as fullback. But that's not all. Eddy had established himself as plain good, all the way.

You can believe the big man's announcement went through our team like wildfire. In what must have been only a few seconds, the whispered decision made its way to all of us.

"Hey guys, wait till the steaks come. Then we all get up and leave. He won't feed Eddy, we won't eat his steaks."

And we didn't.

Love, Grandpa

P.S. We all agreed: Hamburgers at that truckstop down the road never tasted so good.

Judge not by what you have accomplished,
but by what you have become.

The Rodeo Committee Takes Its Stand

Dear A to Z:

This is a story about an individual you couldn't help but like. Everywhere he goes, he's known as "Boss Man."

That's his nickname, of course, but he deserves the moniker. He's a student in an agricultural college. Top grades. Very smart. A natural leader.

Every year the Ag students put on a first-class rodeo, very first class. They bring in professional bronco riders, bull riders, calf ropers, barrel racers. They have it all.

Their rodeo goes three nights in a row, with fifteen thousand total attendance. A gala event, under the complete direction of the Ag students. The purpose? To raise thousands of dollars in scholarship money.

I've been fortunate to know many cowboys and cowgirls in my eighty-two years. And believe me, this crowd is a class act all the way. Plus very religious, which is why I'm often asked to be with them. It's also why I'm writing this letter.

Two years ago "Boss Man" was an underclassman. But even then he was one of the formative leaders. This year he was the chairman.

Each night the rodeo opened with a most unique scene. Suddenly all lights dim except for the spotlight at ring center. Then comes a handsome cowboy on his beautiful spotted horse.

"Good evening, friends," he says. "We're glad you're here. Will you please bow your heads for a word of prayer?" And five thousand heads bow as the cowboy prays.

Then comes the rodeo. Ultra professional. Ultra well received. And when it's over, five thousand people stand to cheer their appreciation.

Now hear this. After their first night's high-quality performance a representative of the school came to the committee. "I've come," he said, "to do a retake with you folks on your prayer before the rodeo. As you know, we're a state institution and you're aware of the Supreme Court ruling: 'No prayers at any events in government buildings.'"

All right, what would you do? What would the committee do? Almost as if by a hidden signal, they turned to "Boss Man" and the "Boss Man" spoke.

"Sir," he began, "we respect your position. We understand you are saying what you've been told to say. But, sir, there is not a single man, not a single woman here, who will agree with your position. If you were riding a bucking bronco; if you were trying to stay on the back of a bull; if you were roping a calf riding as fast as your horse could go; you most certainly would want someone praying for you. Therefore I can tell you right now, the unanimous decision of this committee.

"You do know, I suppose, that this rodeo raises thousands of dollars each year for our school's agricultural scholarships. With that in mind, please report our attitude back to whoever sent you. And do make this clear: if we cannot pray at will and without interference, it will be necessary for us to take our rodeo elsewhere. Which, of course, would mean that the money we raise goes with us.

"You, sir, are in the company of a group where God is an absolute. Thank you for coming. Goodnight."

What do you think happened? What happened is that nothing happened. Each year the rodeo goes on for three nights in its old familiar setting. Same scholarships for the agricultural students. Same prayer. And all because the same kind of young believers took their stand for the Lord.

The story you have just read is true. How do I know? I know because I was there. I am now and always have been a rodeo supporter, a rodeo enthusiast.

So let's have one more authentic "Hurrah" for today's young people. And take it one more time from this old Grandpa:

> The positives of our nation's youth
> far outweigh the negatives;
> and because this is true
> "of his kingdom there shall be no end" (LUKE 1:33).
>
> Love, Grandpa

> It is not enough to be shaking your head
> when you should be raising your voice.

Part Ten

∞

THEN CAME THE WIND AND A DRIVING RAIN

There will be times when
we feel the whole world
is a happy hayride ...
but you fell off back there
somewhere.

$\mathscr{A}$ Lesson from the Swiss Ironmaster

Dear A to Z:

In one town where we lived there was an unusual house. It was built by a man who had more money than he knew what to do with. So he decided to build a giant home for himself.

This rich man's idea about beauty was iron here, iron there, iron, iron everywhere. Great iron fences, massive iron doors, iron bars at the windows, iron railings. And to work up all this iron, he sent to Switzerland for an ironmaster.

On the day he arrived, the ironmaster gathered all his workmen together and made this speech. "Gentlemen, we have a rule we must work by.

"IF YOU WANT A ROUND PIECE OF IRON, TAKE A SQUARE PIECE AND POUND IT ROUND. IF IT'S A SQUARE PIECE YOU ARE NEEDING, TAKE A ROUND PIECE AND POUND IT SQUARE. *FOR IT IS ONLY BY POUNDING THAT IRON GETS CHARACTER.*"

I'm sure you'll agree. What the man said will take a lot of thinking, won't it? Maybe a lifetime.

Love, Grandpa

Remember:
Sometimes awful
happenings and
even tragedies
turn around to bless us.

$\mathcal{H}$e Lost His Arm,
But Wouldn't Give Up

Dear A to Z:

Andy was a young farmer and an active member in one of my rural churches. You would have liked him.

I spent many hours at Andy's place. Helped him feed his cattle, groom the horses, and watch the pigs devour their food.

Andy had a wonderful family. Rhoda was beautiful, and his three children were extra special, too. Theirs was the perfect example of life as it ought to be.

But ...

> *"Then came the wind and a driving rain*
> *And life was never the same again."*

Andy lost his right arm in a corn shelling accident. Somehow his glove got caught in the turning grinder, and it was awful.

What can a young farmer do with one arm? Not much. Cut down to half his working capabilities, he is literally wiped out of his future, finished as a farmer.

Yes, it was one sad day when Andy sold his farm. Everything was auctioned off, including the children's ponies. The cattle, the hogs, his beautiful Percheron horses, machinery: all of it. That new tractor he loved, and Rhoda's prize chickens: they went, too.

Now what would you do? Most of the money from the sale

went to pay the debts, especially the bank. Say it again: one awful, awful day. How do I know? I was there. I looked over and saw Andy and Rhoda holding hands, crying. And yes, I cried, too.

Ask yourself again, "What would I do? Would I quit trying? Give up living? Take my own life?"

What did Andy do? He packed his family in the car and set out across country. Somewhere, somehow, there had to be a way he could start over. You can believe it was one sad day for this young pastor, too. We were such good friends. Would we ever see each other again?

We did.

Eighteen years later, Andy phoned one day and said, "Charlie, you and Martha come see us."

So, we took off for the southern Texas citrus country. Oranges and grapefruit. Great rows of green trees, loaded with rich, yellow fruit. This was Andy and Rhoda's place. This great sprawling citrus orchard was theirs. All of it, theirs.

And their children? The boys were away at college. Leah was in nursing school. All doing well, extra well. Sometimes wind and a driving rain will have a super positive effect on children too.

You get the message, don't you? The Bible says, "All things work together for good to them that love God, to them who are called according to his purpose" (Romans 8:28).

Don't you wish everyone who goes through personal tragedy could have such a happy ending? Of course, you do, and especially if it's you and yours. But you know it doesn't work that way for everyone. Yet it does end like this for some, and that's worth remembering, isn't it?

Turn the camera back now to Andy and his former pastor. The two of us are standing in his orchard, under a heavy-laden orange tree. Yes, as was our custom, we'd been praying. And now he turns to me with tears in his eyes.

"Charlie," he says, "I know you must be thinking what I think every day. If I hadn't lost my arm, look what we'd have missed. I wish everyone could one day have it like Rhoda and I have it. But I feel so sorry for the ones who aren't blessed like we are. You know, for them I'd like to think this could be true: *The ones who hurt and never do have it better here will have it better again in heaven.* Do you think they will, Charlie?"

Yes, I think they will.

Love, Grandpa

"Do You Need a Little Boy to Love?"

Dear A to Z:

One day a little boy knocked at the teacher's front door. She was retired and her name was "Miss Fanchon." She'd never been married so everyone called her an old maid. But all those who knew her, loved her.

So here I was at her door asking, "I know a little boy who needs someone to love him. Do you need a little boy to love?"

"Oh, yes, I do," she answered. "Very much I do. Come in and be my little boy. We'll have some hot chocolate and cookies. Then I'll show you my canaries."

Miss Fanchon was famous for her canaries. "Best canaries in all northern Iowa." That's what everyone said, and she showed me the secret.

Whenever her young canaries grew enough to make noises, she started them singing. First, she would put the young canary alone in a cage and cover the cage with black cloth. Then she moved the young canary's cage over beside one of her very best singers. And that was the secret.

How long would she leave this little canary alone in the darkness? Answer: for a long, long time. Just imagine you were that canary. You didn't have anything else to do, so wouldn't you begin to sing? Yes, you'd learn to sing exactly like the singing you heard. Keep singing, day after day after day. And wonder of wonders, one day you'd become a champion singer, too. Naturally then, when somebody came to buy you, they'd pay the highest price. And, of course, you would go on singing your best for your new owners.

How many times did I knock on Miss Fanchon's door? How many times did I drink her hot chocolate, eat her cookies, and listen to her life story? Many, many times.

Years and years ago she had been in love with a wonderful classmate. They started in kindergarten together, best friends. Then, when they were old enough, they became sweethearts. But here it is again:

> *"Then came the wind and a driving rain*
> *And life was never the same again."*

So sad. Miss Fanchon's sweetheart went to war and never came back.

Oh, Miss Fanchon, thank you for the love you gave this little boy. Thank you for all your hot chocolate and cookies. Thank you for all you taught me. But mostly thank you for teaching me this:

> *Canaries that sing in the dark can become*
> *the very best canaries.*

Love, Grandpa

— ∞ —

Whosoever shall receive one such little child in my name receiveth me.

MATTHEW 18:5

— ∞ —

The Touchdown Nobody Saw

---- ∞ ----

Dear A to Z:

We were playing Eldora for the league title. And would you believe? After the first quarter it began to snow. I don't mean one of those nice, soft snows. This was a genuine blizzard. Snow coming down heavy, heavy. So heavy we could barely see the opposition, or even our teammates.

Would they call the game off? No. In Iowa they don't call off games for snow. Especially not championship games, so let's get on with it. And we did.

It wasn't much fun, of course. And one reason was that most of the fans had left by now. Except for a few loyal parents and girlfriends like Martha, plus the referees.

Hardly any way for anyone to score, except perhaps by luck or something unexpected. And that's what happened. We had the ball right now and our quarterback called "Tackle Eligible." On this play, one end moves over beside the other end. Almost always a fooler. Why? Because nobody is expecting the tackle to catch a pass. Yet he really is eligible. And this time it was Charlie.

I caught the ball and took off in the snow. Nobody watching, except for one person. Lucky me, lucky us, the referee happened to be right there beside me and saw it all.

So off we went, the two of us, for a touchdown. The winning touchdown, and I, Charlie the tackle, made it. Yes, the Conference

Championship was won, but nobody saw who the hero was. Our coach hadn't seen it, my fellow teammates hadn't seen it, and Martha hadn't seen it.

Oh, glorious sight. Oh, poor Charlie. A real thriller, except for one thing. Nobody could see it.

Do you see any lessons here worth pondering? I do now. But you can believe they were a long time coming. Yet they really were worth learning, so I'll share them with you.

One: To live only for grandstand cheering is a grave mistake. The deeper satisfactions of life do come when WE know we've done a good job.

Two: The Lord is never blinded by snow or any storm of any kind. He knows when we've done a good thing and his knowing really is what matters most for now and forever.

Love, Grandpa

$\mathcal{A}$ Legend of the Indian Chiefs

Dear A to Z:

The Indian warriors from many tribes were sitting around their campfire. This was one of their most important gatherings ever. They'd been at war against each other for many moons. But too many of their young braves had gone to the Happy Hunting Ground. Killed in battle.

Not good, of course. So now they were putting an end to the war, smoking their peace pipes.

As all men do at their gatherings, each chief was bragging about his own son's bravery. Chief after chief told his proud story, but the Old Chief said nothing. So when all had finished their stories, they prompted their leader. Would he speak now? And he would.

"My son," said the Great One, "did not go to war."

"And why not?" came the cry of surprise.

"Listen," said the Old Chief, "and I will explain.

"Before the war began, my son was down in the canyon. He had gone there to study the wild horses. Many horses. But he is wise. He studied their habits. Studied their movements. Then when he knew the way, he drove them home to our corral. All by himself he did this."

"Oh," they said in unison, "that's good."

"No," said the Great Chief, "that's bad."

"And why," they asked in unison, "why is that bad?"

150

"Because," came the reply, "when he was training the wild horses, one mighty stallion threw him and broke my son's leg."

"Oh," they said again together, "that's bad."

"No," said the Wise One, "that's good."

And once more they asked, "Why is that good?"

"That's good because he made a decision. Since he was unable to fight, he would go to the university and study to become a doctor."

"Oh," they cried, "that's good."

"No," came the Old Chief's retort, "that's bad."

"Why is that bad?"

"That's bad," he answered, "because his mother and I miss him so."

"Oh, this we understand," they said again, "that's bad."

"No," said the Great One, smiling, "that's good."

"That's good you say? Why good?"

"That's good because his mother and I can run around the teepee any way we want. We are free and this is good. Very good."

Time to end this story. And knowing you as I do, I am sure you are both SMART enough and WISE enough to draw your own lessons on this one.

Love, Grandpa

Part Eleven

——— ∞ ———

LOVE, COURTSHIP, AND MARRIAGE

$\mathcal{A}$ young man took his bride to a famous beach for their honeymoon. On the first afternoon, as they strolled beside the water, he waxed poetic. Dramatically pointing a hand over the sea, he intoned, "Roll on thou vast and deep blue ocean, roll!"

Whereupon his young bride threw her arms around her husband and, with deep emotion, exclaimed, "Oh, Richard dear. Look how wonderful you are. It's doing it!"

*W*hen Will We Know *All* About Each Other?

Dear A to Z:

Larry and Jennifer came to see me yesterday. They have been going together two years, and they've set their date. Next month.

Larry is a brilliant physician. Jennifer is a high-tech computer specialist. Everyone thinks they're great together, and you should see them. Smiling, laughing, having fun, but sometimes ultra-serious, too.

This was one of their ultra-serious times. They'd come to tell me they were getting nervous. So could they share one question bothering them?

"Certainly," I said. "What is the question?"

"Just how well should we know each other before we're married? You and Martha lived together forty-eight years, didn't you? So how long did it take before you knew each other completely?"

There is only one possible answer to their question, and that is the single word: *Never.*

When you are ready for marriage, the words are not, "We know all about each other now."

Instead, as you come to the altar, the two of you (being WISE) will be praying together:

Lord, one reason we wish to be married
is that we see so many wonderful things
in each other
it will take us a lifetime
to know them all.
Thank you, Lord, for love so exciting, so divine.

For each of you I wish that kind of love.

Love, Grandpa

There be three things which are too wonderful for me, yea, four which I know not: The way of an eagle in the air; the way of a serpent upon a rock; the way of a ship in the midst of the sea; and the way of a man with a maid.

PROVERBS 30:18-19

Summer 'Em and Winter 'Em Again

Dear A to Z:

It was a university banquet in Kansas. The beautiful young lady sitting next to me was a senior about to graduate. Her name plate read "class president," and I wasn't surprised. She looked like a leader, acted like a leader, talked like a leader. Her name was Norah, which means "Decision." A very good name for someone in her position, wasn't it?

I noticed that she was constantly looking at the main door entrance. Over and over she turned and looked, turned and looked.

Finally I whispered, "Norah, I bet I can guess what's going on in your pretty head. Want me to tell you?" Yes, she wanted me to tell her, so I did. And I was right.

She was looking for her sweetheart. His name was Bernie, and he went to State College down the road. He said he'd be late tonight and she was getting nervous. She wanted so much for him to be here when she gave her welcome address.

Then at last, he arrived. A handsome young man, exactly what you'd expect for someone like Norah. Unfortunately he couldn't sit with us because our table was for the participants. So Norah and I were free to carry on our discussion.

She began by telling me how much Bernie meant to her. There was no doubt, she said, about his feelings. Fact is, he wanted very much to marry this spring. Yet somehow she still wasn't quite sure. So, she'd been talking with her grandmother.

"And what did your grandmother tell you?"

"Well, when I told her I wasn't quite sure she said: 'Honey, what you should do with Bernie is just like what we did with our sheep. You remember how we'd summer them on grass? Then in the winter we'd put them in the barns and fatten them for market. Most of them would be ready to go by spring. But there were always a few needing more time. So we'd summer 'em and winter 'em again.'"

Norah paused, then spoke again quietly. "Then she told me maybe that's what I should do with Bernie. What do you think?"

What would you have told her? Probably something exactly like I told her:

"You are a very *smart* young lady, Norah. And your grandmother is a very *wise* grandmother."

Love, Grandpa

Always a basic question for lovers is: Are we held together by the gravitation of curiosity or loneliness, or by the everlasting gravitation of God's love for us and in us?

When Is It Time to Change a Dream?

Dear A to Z:

A certain timid young man fell in love with Babbette, the high school prom queen. So, after he had dated her for a time, he proposed.

"No, Melvin," she said. "I cannot marry you until you have made us a fortune. So, you go out into the world and come back with one million dollars. Then I will marry you."

So off he went but, sorry to say, he was a long time gone. A long, long time. Christmas came and went. No Melvin. No million dollars. The alumni dances at graduation; plus June and its many weddings. But poor Babbette, always a bridesmaid, never a bride.

Then one night came a knock on her door. Who do you suppose it was? Yes, you're right. Melvin.

"Oh, Melvin!" she screamed. "Come in! Come in, my darling. So much I have missed you. And how did you do with our goal, sweetheart?"

Alas, twisting his cap, shuffling his feet, and very near tears, he said, "Honest, Babbette, I did try. Ever so hard I tried. But all I could save was eighty-nine cents."

Now, opening the door wider, in most fervent tones, she said softly, "Oh, Melvin. That's near enough. Come in, come in."

And what, do you suppose, is the lesson here?

Love, Grandpa

— ∞ —

Receive my instruction, and not silver;
and knowledge rather than choice gold.
For wisdom is better than rubies;
and all the things that may be desired
are not to be compared to it.

PROVERBS 8:10-11

— ∞ —

"How Do I Know if I'm Really in Love?"

Dear A to Z:

Many years ago I wrote a column for Teen magazine. I received countless letters in response to my column, but one kind far outnumbered the others. And this is that kind:

Jimmy and I have never dated anyone else. For three years we've been going steady, and we don't see how we can possibly be married for at least two more years. All my friends and even my parents say it's not smart to only go with one person. You know what I mean? They ask questions like, "How can you possibly know you're right for each other if you don't date around and evaluate others? You could be making a big mistake." So tell me. How do I know if I'm really in love?

Fact: No author, no counselor, no expert, no grandpa knows all there is to know about real love. That being true, you'll want to think and think, study and study, pray and pray.

You realize I couldn't possibly answer today's question in one letter. But I could give you further help if you need more help in your thinking. Some years ago I wrote a book entitled, *How to Know If You're Really in Love*. That book is divided into "Ten

Tests for the Real Thing." And here they are:

1. **The Transparency Test:** Do you find it easy to be open with the other person? To share your ideas, your fears, your dreams?

2. **The Liberty Test:** Are you both free to be who you really are? Or does one partner want to dominate?

3. **The Unselfishness Test:** Are you willing to give the other person what he or she needs? Even when it's hard or inconvenient, are you willing to adjust?

4. **The Mercy Test:** When one partner does something wrong, does the other forgive willingly and completely, without holding grudges?

5. **The Apology Test:** When arguments develop, are both parties willing to say, "I'm sorry I hurt you. Please forgive me"?

6. **The Sexuality Test:** Do you treat each other with respect, with genuine affection and purity?

7. **The Money Test:** Do you have similar viewpoints on how to spend money, including how much to save and how much to give?

8. **The Distance Test:** When you are apart from each other for a time, do you become anxious or suspicious? Or can you relax and trust God to take care of things until you can be together again?

9. **The Fun Test:** Do you enjoy each other's company, even when you're doing everyday things?

10. **The Holiness Test:** Does your friendship bring you closer to God? Do you pray together? Are you better for having this person in your life?

Giant questions we're dealing with here, aren't they? So keep thinking. Keep talking. Keep praying. And say it one more time: This is one place where we need to be both *SMART* and *WISE*.

Love, Grandpa

Editor's note: If you would like a copy of Dr. Shedd's book, *How Can We Know if We're Really in Love?*, see the final page of this book.

Secrets from the Best Marriage Ever

Dear A to Z:

Here is an ancient Chinese proverb for our consideration: "Every one on earth is like the line of a poem going through the world, looking for the one line with which it can rhyme."

Do you believe that? I don't, because I think it's too limited. But this I do believe:

> Marriage is not so much FINDING the right person
> as it is BEING the right person.

My Martha believed that, too, and because we wanted to BE right for each other we made some specific commitments. Commitments like these two:

Number One: *Every day we will pay each other a compliment.*

A simple, "I like you because ..." It could even be something we'd said before. "Because of your laugh." "The touch of your hand." "The way I look up from the paper and you're smiling at me."

On and on, day after day, this was the rule. We owed each other at least one compliment every twenty-four hours. We called it our "I like you because" agreement.

When we were first married, the popular term for compliments was "warm fuzzies." And we never gave up using that term. At night before we went to sleep, let's say one of us hadn't lived up to this agreement. So? So the other person would say: "I haven't had my 'warm fuzzy' today."

Stop what you're thinking, Charlie. Nothing is more important than this. You owe her a warm fuzzy. What a way of drifting off together!

Number Two: *Every week we would pay each other a NEW compliment.*

And I do mean *brand* new. It had to be something we'd never said before. A new gift of love exchanged, person to person, every week. And what do you think that would do to the memories? Take it from this old grandpa, that kind of bank to draw on is absolutely awesome.

Martha went to heaven ten years ago. But she went to heaven knowing two thousand four hundred and ninety-six things I liked about her. And could I possibly go on alone in my life without those two thousand four hundred and ninety-six things I know she liked about me? Ah, love with praise, how beautiful it is.

Have you ever heard the old folk song, "Where Have All the Flowers Gone?" Sad title, isn't it? But in how many marriages does the record play? Answer: In too, too many.

It's *SMART* to remember this: Nobody, including your mate, ever gets too much, "I like you because ..."

Love, Grandpa

A word fitly spoken is like apples of gold in pictures of silver."

PROVERBS 25:11

Part Twelve

---∞---

HAPPINESS IS A FUN FAMILY

In the house of the righteous is much treasure: but in the revenues of the wicked is trouble.

PROVERBS 15:6

$\mathcal{W}$hat Three Words Best Describe Your Family?

Dear A to Z:

Here we are, back at our early letters. Only this time I'm asking you to broaden your word choices. Today it's you and the folks you live with. Here we go for another selection of words.

Remember this before you start: We all have good days, we all have bad days. Uppers and downers are a part of every family. But think now of the family's overall days, and focus on the week by week feelings, your month by month attitudes. Now what words best describe your family? This, of course, means you'll be grading yourself too.

Three words that best describe our family are:

_____, _____, _____

Would your family enjoy a discussion of the three words you chose? Or better still, ask each member of your family to pick three words, too. (And be sure you say a special prayer before you start sharing.)

Result? You could have (a) some big-time fun; (b) some very interesting insights straight from each other; (c) some possible adjustments to bless everyone in your family.

Remember: The more your family knows what others in the family really think, the healthier your family will be.

Love, Grandpa

"Now, Everybody Tell Your Most Interesting Thing"

Dear A to Z:

What are the three most important words in family life? Are they, "I love you," "Please forgive me," or "You are beautiful"? All good choices for sure, but here's my nomination. The three most important words are actually one word, three times: "Talk, talk, talk."

You can see immediately why these three words are important. Without talk the "I love you's" will not get through. Neither will the "Please forgive me's" or the "You are beautiful's."

So what can we do to promote "talk, talk, talk"?

Here's what we did. Every evening meal featured a fun item called, "Most Interesting Things." Right after the blessing it would begin. Every member of the family would participate, and the conversation might run something like this:

"My most interesting thing is that we got a new girl in our class and is she ever cute."

"I hit a home run today and we won the game."

"Danny told me his mother has cancer. Isn't that awful?"

"I saw a rainbow on the way home."

"I got a D in Algebra and I'm so scared. How will I ever make it?" ... and on and on from fun to fear, from glad to sad, to anything of any kind. No limits.

You see what's happening, don't you? Everyone in the family is sharing a little bit of their own mind and heart.

Try it, keep it up for thirty days, and you'll never be without it. Why? Because sharing like this will meld your family into a beautiful oneness.

Love, Grandpa

P.S. I forgot to tell you, if you don't feel like saying anything tonight that's OK. All you have to do is put a quarter in a "penalty box." When there are enough quarters, use them for a family fun time!

"If We Didn't Have Daddy ..."

———— ∞ ————

Dear A to Z:

Here's another grandpa wish for you.

I wish for you the happy memories of happy conversation at your happy dinner table.

At our house we had this after-dinner rule. Everyone stayed around for some fun talk after we'd eaten. Is there anything more beautiful than a family chattering, laughing, sharing together? I loved these times, loved the memories they produced.

Plus I loved something else. I loved the chance to clean up everyone's leftovers.

One night as I was grazing from plate to plate during conversation time, Paul (age 7) came out with this classic:

*"Hey, I just thought of something. If we **didn't have Daddy**, we'd have to keep a pig."*

Laugh, laugh, laugh. I wish you could have heard the laughter. And what could a daddy do when the whole family went jolly up? Nothing but laugh with them.

I hope you have a bunch of fun around your dinner table. I hope you can laugh at yourself sometimes. And I hope your family feels they can laugh at you too.

Keep laughing.

Love, Grandpa

Our Fifty-Fifty Disaster Deal

———— ∞ ————

Dear A to Z:

Experts tell us it's important to make children responsible for their carelessness. Agreed. You did it, you pay for it. Or is there a better way?

We decided there might be a better way. How about sharing the disasters? Some folks call them "calamities." But by any other name a mess-up is a mess-up. So, can we have an example? Yes. Here are two:

Case one: Karen parked her car one afternoon in a "No Parking" zone. Now why would she do that? Actually the curb markings in our town are not all super clear. And she was in a hurry. Still, *she* got the ticket, didn't she? So who pays the fine?

Karen, but not one hundred percent of it. No, in our family it's Karen and parents together. But why? Because the parents agree: "Since we raised you, there just might have been some flaw in our educational procedures. That being true, we'll go 50-50."

Case two: Paul knocked a baseball through the neighbor's big glass window. You're right, he and his playmates should have known better. Hitting home runs that close to bay windows is not judicious. They know that now. So why rub it in? Paul is a very bright young fifth grader (straight A's all the way); he learns fast. So Paul pays half, we pay half. And for the sake of peace on our block, hurry with the money. These particular neighbors are the screaming kind.

Sometimes at parents' meetings when I describe our fifty-fifty disaster deal I get negative reactions. Why should a parent pay half? It was the child's fault, not yours. If you do too much for them they won't respect you.

What do you think?

Love, Grandpa

— ∞ —

Be kind to one another, tenderhearted, forgiving one another, as God in Christ forgave you.

EPHESIANS 4:32, RSV

— ∞ —

Family Night
Plus One Night out Alone with Dad

Dear A to Z:

They slept beneath the moon
They worked beneath the sun;
They lived a life of "going-to-do"
And died with nothing done.

That's so like too many of us, isn't it? Good intentions do not happy families make. So what's the answer? The answer, Martha and I decided, was to make commitments. To make them and keep them a sacred trust.

Example: One night every week would be "Family Night." And except for emergencies, no excuses. Both for parents and for children, no excuses. Of course, there were times when emergencies did interfere. But if this happened we'd pick a different night.

What did we do on family night? Sometimes we stayed home and played games ... shot baskets ... had discussions ... sang songs ... watched TV (programs chosen by vote) ... laughed ... ate ice cream ... and loved each other.

Then sometimes (by vote again) we'd go out. Out to our favorite hamburger stand ... out for a long ride, for a movie, for a game. No wonder, is it, if you were to ask someone in our family, "What are your favorite memories?", one answer would be "Family Night."

Then, in addition, to this sharing together in the family, we had another time trust:

Every month on a given night, Father and one child would be out together alone. Out for dinner. Out for a long ride. Out for a game, a movie, a shopping spree. (Oh, how we loved those shopping sprees.) And along with all these fun times, you know what else: "Talk, talk, talk." Child to father, father to child: time together, one on one.

Take it from Grandpa, Dear A to Z, one day it will happen. You'll have your own family and you will say: "How could God ever be so good to me?" When you do, be sure to give your family time, sacred time.

Love, Grandpa

Part Thirteen

---- ∞ ----

MANAGING MONEY AND
OTHER ADULT MATTERS

*T*rust in your money

and down you go!

PROVERBS 11:28, LB

*W*hen Will You Get Your Car? And How Will You Know You're Ready for It?

Dear A to Z:

One of the facts of life when it comes to families is that family members need to go places. To ball games, to music lessons, to the mall. Another fact of life is that young people are always in a great hurry to grow up. They are always in a rush to experience life to the fullest, and that means reaching a great rite of passage: getting a driver's license.

Age alone won't tell you when you're ready. Some sixteen-year-olds are both smarter and wiser than some eighteen-year-olds. But here are a few questions to consider, a few tests to help you and your parents decide.

First, the practical and financial questions. Have you saved enough to pay the bills before you get your car? Do you know what it costs for gasoline? What do you know about insurance and upkeep? Will you treat your car as a friend?

Next, the character questions. Do you ask for advice from your parents when you need it? What is your patience quotient and your common-sense factor? In what other ways have you proven your maturity? Will you be grateful enough to respect what you've been trusted with? Are you fully aware of your responsibility to other drivers?

You may be able to think of other questions, too. There are lots of them, on and on adinfinitim.

But that's enough, isn't it? Or is it too much? Whichever it is, here's a true story for you about a girl named Gretchen. I know it's true because I was Gretchen's pastor. She was a beautiful girl, but at fourteen some of her ideas were not very mature. So one night she sneaked out the window and took her father's car for a spin. Whoopee, she was free!

Or was she? I regret to tell you what happened. Not being sure of her driving skills, Gretchen ran head-on into another car. It was awful. Especially it was awful for the parents of that beautiful baby, who were all in the other car. Would the little one live? Would she be all right if she did live?

I am glad to tell you the baby did live. And was I ever proud of Gretchen. Every day, for weeks, she visited the emergency room to see how things were. Every day she met someone from the family, and that was hard. But every day she told them how sorry she was.

How wrong she'd been. Every day she asked the nurses again, "Do you think she'll live?" Gretchen said she'd rather die herself than for that little life to be taken.

Fortunately, the baby *did* live, and Gretchen grew up.

Would you like to guess what Gretchen is doing today? You're right, she's a nurse. She has two children of her own, and whenever she can, she works the baby ward. They tell me she is one of their very best nurses.

Isn't that a happy ending to one awful story? It's almost like a fairy tale, isn't it? But you get the message, don't you?

You are both *smart* and *wise* if you wait your legal turn to drive a car.

Love, Grandpa

$\mathcal{Y}$our Money and the "No Fail" Way to Handle It

Dear A to Z:

If you had three simple "No Fail" rules for handling your money, you'd probably like that, wouldn't you?

Well, I'm about to give you three that worked wonders for one couple I know. For many years they lived by these rules and they were simply super rules for them.

Here are the three rules:

1. Give ten percent.

2. Save ten percent.

3. Spend the rest with thanksgiving and praise.

You try these rules, stick with them, and you will see. It's just like the Good Book says: "For the measure you give will be the measure you get back" (Luke 6:38, RSV).

Love, Grandpa

If You'd Have Put More in You'd Have Got More Out

Dear A to Z:

This was a small country church, so small they couldn't have a full-time pastor. So, every Sunday evening they invited one of the town ministers as their guest preacher. Tonight's choice was everybody's favorite. This would be a fine service.

So now he had arrived, a bit late, but no matter. They took up waiting time with an old-fashioned hymn sing.

What was this new item at the entrance tonight? A small box labeled, "Alms Box" with the words, "Collection Money Here, Please." So the minister reached in his pocket and dropped in fifty cents. Then on to the service.

It was a good service. Good spirit. Good visiting afterward. Then when most of the folks had gone, here came the Finance Chairman.

"Reverend," he said, "As you can see, we've adopted a new policy. From now on we give the contents of this Alms Box to our guest preacher."

Then, taking off the cover, he said, "Put out your hands, please." The preacher did. And can you believe this? Nothing came out but his own fifty-cent piece.

As they were getting in the car to leave for home, guess what happened? Fastening his seat belt, the preacher's little boy said, "Daddy, I just thought of something. *If you'd have put more in you'd have got more out.*"

Love, Grandpa

The Secret to Managing Money God's Way

———— ∞ ————

Dear A to Z:

There is an interesting story about how "Ivory" soap got its name. Harley Proctor was one of the founders of the famous Proctor-Gamble Company. He lived in Ohio during the Civil War.

One day a worker in his factory allowed the soap-making machine to run too long. Because he failed to turn it off, this particular batch of soap was much lighter than usual. When it was made into bars and cakes, the soap floated. The foreman suggested that it be reboiled, but Proctor said, "Maybe somebody will like it."

They did. Customers who were used to fishing for their soap at the bottom of the tub took to it in a big way. They were glad to pay well for the new product.

For a time it was marketed without a name. Nobody could think of a good title for it. Then one Sunday, Harley Proctor heard a hymn at church which gave him an idea.

The song he heard was an oldie about the pure white mansions of heaven. It was entitled, "Out of the Ivory Palaces." He decided right then that since ivory stood for purity this would be a good word for his new product. That's how Ivory Soap and Ivory Flakes got their label.

Harley Proctor was a tither. He set aside ten cents out of every dollar for his church. As he prospered he gradually increased his percentage and gave it to good causes until he was finally giving more than he was keeping.

There are many people in the world today who live by the rule of the tithe. They have studied the Bible and believe God calls them to do this. They have also learned by practical experience that the Scripture means what it says when it keeps repeating the theme that no one can ever out-give God!

Sounds crazy, doesn't it? You give more away and you have more to give? But what does the Book of Life promise? "Give and it shall be given unto you!" ... "As ye sow, so shall ye also reap!" ... "Cast thy bread on the waters and after many days it shall return unto thee!"

One of life's most common complaints these days is that there just isn't enough money to go around. How can we correct this constant problem? Most of us have been oriented in the thought that the solution is to increase the intake. What if we have been concentrating too hard on the wrong end?

Question for serious meditation on me and my money: *"Would the divine Giver be pouring more into my life if I was pouring more out of my life to bless the world?"*

Love, Grandpa

Part Fourteen

— ∞ —

HAPPINESS IS BEING
BEST FRIENDS WITH THE LORD

My God and I

These words were given to me one day when I asked God to remind me of the words to the original hymn.

My God and I, we walk the hills together.
My God and I, we walk so tenderly.
We climb the mounts of sorrow,
    pain and trouble.
My God and I, we walk unendingly.

We do not know the joy that comes
    with riches.
We do not care that pleasure comes with fame.
We only know we talk life's trail together.
My God and I, still will we walk the same.

And though I've sinned, he knows each
    fallen moment.
And though I've erred, he cares enough for me
To wash me clean of every stain and evil.
My God and I, we walk forgivingly.

Last Eve I Paused Before the Blacksmith's Door

Dear A to Z:

Do you have favorite places where you like to go?

One of my boyhood favorite places was the village blacksmith shop.

Does that seem strange? Looking back, it seems strange even to me. But in the little town where I lived there were not many interesting places.

So off we would go to the blacksmith shop. My buddies were eight-year-old twins, and I was almost eight. Day after day we would sit on the blacksmith's bench and watch "Smithy" at work. Nice nickname, isn't it? Smithy.

There he would be all day, mending broken tractors, mending big machines, mending little machines, mending tools, big and little. Hammer, hammer, hammer. Shape, shape, shape. Wipe the sweat off and do it again.

In the center of his shop there was a place Smithy called his "forge." Every day and all day long he kept a red-hot fire going. Why? To form exactly the right shoes for his animal customers. To heat all kinds of metal pieces for machinery repairs.

But every now and then the blacksmith had what he called his "time out" moments. He told us these times were an absolute must because blacksmithing was hard, hard work. And it could be dangerous. Especially with the animals. Horses, mules, ponies, and ox teams are all alike here. They do not take to someone pounding on their feet. And dangerous, too, were broken pieces of machinery flying loose.

So now comes what we liked the very best about "our" blacksmith shop. Because he loved children, Smithy would sit and visit, have a cold drink, and rest. But he would also give us a cold drink, so this was a very special time. Of course, nobody but the blacksmith and his helper were permitted beyond the door. So "our" blacksmith built a bench. A very nice metal bench, with padding. His special gift, just for us. He called it our "pew" and he smiled when he said, "You're my weektime congregation."

Why would he call us that? Because this blacksmith was also a preacher. He pastored a small church out in the country. Non-denominational, mostly older folks, and very few children. I think that may be why he loved to see us come, loved to have us there, loved to talk with us, loved to teach us.

He would teach us Bible lessons I have never forgotten. He taught us songs and sang them with us. Songs for sharing, poems for sharing with others, and here's one I know you'll like. Straight from a small-town Smithy, just for you. No, he didn't write it, and it was so old nobody seems to know who did. But I think you'll agree, this author was very special.

Last eve I paused before the blacksmith's door
And heard the anvil ring the vesper chime.
Then looking in I saw upon the floor,
Old hammers worn with beating years of time.

"How many anvils have you had?" said I,
"To wear and batter all these hammers so."
"Just one," the Smith replied,
"The anvil wears the hammers out, you know."

And so I thought, how like God's Word
For ages skeptic blows have beat upon.
Yet still throughout the world is heard,
"The anvil is unworn, the hammers gone."

Beautiful, isn't it? This might be another one to learn and write on your heart.

Love, Grandpa

"The Call of the Lord"

———— ∞ ————

Dear A to Z:

This was the Iowa State Oratorical contest. Twelve of us from different colleges were about to compete.

What is "oratory"? The dictionary defines oratory as "an elaborate discourse delivered in a formal and dignified manner." Back in my college days "oratory" was big-time competition.

So here we were at one of our Midwestern colleges, ready to compete. There were five judges, four men and one woman, all faculty members from different schools.

"So let's get started. First we will draw for order of appearance." That did make a difference, because each speaker could leave when finished. For results, read tomorrow morning's paper. But, alas, poor Charlie drew number twelve. Meaning, of course, I would hear eleven brilliant speakers. Every one on themes like armament, immigration, the Supreme Court, tariffs, limiting congressional terms, et cetera, et cetera. Very heady stuff.

At last it was my turn, but we were considerably over our adjournment time. The judges were looking at their watches and I didn't blame them. I could almost hear their private thoughts: "OK, kid. Cut it short. We've heard enough."

You can imagine I felt exactly like those five judges: enough is enough. But something other than weariness was bothering me. My speech sounded so plain-vanilla after all I'd heard. Honestly, I was almost tempted to say, "Let's forget it. I've got a date. I want to go home."

Instead what I said was something like this:

"With all due respect to you, Judges, you look exactly like I feel. Exhausted. My mind is spinning with all these brilliant presentations. Weren't they amazing? Such awesome subjects. And here I stand with my talk about a football coach."

The lady judge brightened considerably at this. "What? You don't mean it. Football? That's my game. My husband was an All-American center. I can't believe this. At least one thing today I'll understand," she laughed.

Whereupon the other judges laughed too and joined the sentiment with something like, "Amen. Let's go for it."

So, I began:

"Nestled back among the hills of Christiana, Norway, lies the little hamlet of Voss. A plain and ordinary village, but not at all plain and ordinary in its gift to us. I present to you now, the greatest gridiron coach of all time. Knute Rockne, idol of American football."

Modesty forbids me telling who won the state oratorical contest that year. And what did I learn? For one thing, I learned why two men were sitting at the back of our room. All day long they'd been there, taking notes, looking at each other, nodding sometimes. Shaking their heads sometimes.

After I'd heard the judges' verdict and thanked them, I headed for the door. I had a date with Martha tomorrow morning and I could hardly wait. I'd be driving most of the night to get there.

But here they came, these two mysterious men. Introducing themselves, they asked, "Can we take you to dinner?"

Well, I was hungry. And in addition to that I was curious. "Who are you? What do you do?"

Over dinner they answered my questions. The men were representatives of a major American business conglomerate. Producers and marketers of lumber, metals, rubber, jewelry, and other items. So why were they here? They were scouts for their company. Scouts looking for young men who could be trained as court lawyers. Men to defend them in lawsuits. Men who would save them big money. "Would you be interested, Charlie?"

I certainly would. Three full years of law school, all expenses paid. Housing. Automobile. Plus a monthly stipend sufficient to be married.

"Then sign right here on the dotted line."

You can imagine I wanted to sign before they changed their minds. "But you see, gentlemen. I have a girlfriend back in our home town. I need to talk it over with her."

So there we sat, Martha and I, in our favorite hideaway high up above the city. See those lights of downtown and the moon shining on our river. What a place for me to tell my favorite girl the weekend happenings, to share my exciting news. And think what all this offer can mean to us. Security. Excitement. The finest of everything. And above all, we could get married right away.

She was so excited. So proud. So loving. Dream on, young couple. What a future.

Then it was time to go home and, as usual, we had our prayer together. Always that was a beautiful part of our "Good-bye. Thank you, Sweetheart. See you tomorrow." Only this time before we said goodnight, there was an addition to the conversation.

"Charlie," she began, "I hardly know whether to tell you what I'm thinking right now. I don't *want* to tell you, but I think I should. You know how we've talked about you maybe being a minister. Well, when you were almost through telling me about what happened today, it was almost as if suddenly I heard a voice. From way down inside or off there somewhere I heard it. And I am going to tell you what I heard. What I heard was this:

"Martha, right now you must ask Charlie:
'Charlie, if you'd be worth all this
to that company,
what do you suppose you might be worth
to the Lord?'"

Three years later I became a minister, and Martha became a minister's wife. Three years later. Yes, it was a long three years to wait for our wedding, but we both knew it was right.

Love, Grandpa

P.S. Remember dear A to Z: It is smart to consider all your talents as you plan your future. It is also smart to evaluate the various offers coming your way. But you will remember, won't you? Wise people always take things up first with the Lord.

And we know that in all things God works for the good of those who love him.
ROMANS 8:28, NIV

Prayer, Church, and Heaven Hereafter

———— ∞ ————

Dear A to Z:

It was bedtime for little Ronnie. So here they were in his room—Ronnie and his grandmother. Now he knelt and began his goodnight prayer. This was a regular ritual, every night. Grandma would sit beside him while he prayed. Usually she could understand each word, but not tonight. Ronnie was almost whispering some things.

"Ronnie," she said in her usual gentle voice. "Tonight, I'm not hearing you. Can you speak a little louder?"

Whereupon Ronnie raised his head, smiled, and said, "Grandma, I wasn't speaking to you. God is my best friend. Sometimes we only talk to each other."

It is my hope for you, dear A to Z, that you and the Lord will always be best friends. Yes, the kind of friends who share some things, just the two of you. And I hope that friendship lasts forever.

In our final letters we'll take a look at these three all-important meeting places with the Lord.

PRAYER
CHURCH
and HEAVEN

Love, Grandpa

Prayer

— ∞ —

$\mathcal{W}$here do we look for God? You don't have to look very far. Listen to the words of Jesus:

"Behold, I stand at the door and knock: if any man hear my voice, and open the door, I will come in to him, and will sup with him, and he with me."

REVELATION 3:20

What Do You Think of First Thing in the Morning?

Dear A to Z:

When you wake up and your brain begins turning over, what is your number one thought?

I once had the fun of writing a national newspaper column for *Teen* magazine. One of the funnest items was asking young people to share their wake-up thoughts. A flood of answers came, like this:

"Oh, no. It can't be time to get up already.... Wonder what mood my parents are in.... and my English teacher, will there be another of her awful tests?... Wonder what Mom has for breakfast.... Where did I leave my chewing gum?... Suppose my boyfriend will call me today?... Hear that? It's my brother in the bathroom.... Will one good thing happen today? I doubt it." On and on, seriatim and in extenso.

Those last two words, "seriatim" and "in extenso" are fun old timers. Look them up. Finding new words (and new meanings to old words) will give you a special inner glow.

Martha and I had a special way to open our day, every day. I have always been an early riser. But Martha was one hundred and eighty degrees the opposite. So when we did see each other every morning, we would hold hands and say together:

"This is the day which the Lord hath made;
we will rejoice and be glad in it."   PSALMS 118:24

197

There was one more thing we did in our early wake-up hours. This was a prayer, a simple prayer, but oh so meaningful. And this was the prayer:

"What can we do for you today, Lord?"

Now that prayer is an awesome prayer if you say it and mean what you say. Fits right in with our opening theme, doesn't it? "Be What You Is."

And what is "You"? You is a creation of the Lord, created for his purposes. If that is true, could there ever be a better prayer than this?

"Lord, since you made me, you know better than anyone what I should do and be. So guide me, Lord, every day and all the time. I want to do what I can for you.... Amen."

Love, Grandpa

The Lady Who Prayed for Her Plants and Flowers

Dear A to Z:

The Bible says, "In everything by prayer and supplication with thanksgiving let your requests be made known to God" (Philippians 4:6, RSV).

EVERYTHING? YES, EVERYTHING.

A lady I know prayed every day for her plants and flowers. And what happened? What happened is that she had the most wonderful garden you could ever imagine. Plus the most beautiful flowers you would ever see. Plus she had such a productive garden she had enough to share with everyone: friends, neighbors, hospitals, the church. Plus you, too, if you'd lived anywhere near her.

She didn't make a big scene of this. But everyday, there she would be, going from row to row, praying. Sure, some people thought that was somewhat strange. But that didn't bother her. She went right on praying for her cucumbers and corn, her cabbage and carrots. Plus all kinds of other things that didn't start with "c." Such as her watermelons. Oh, her watermelons.

Like I said, some people wondered about her. But not I. Whenever I saw her out there in the garden praying, I thought: "This is the most beautiful woman God ever created."

And her name was Martha.

Love, Grandpa

"Da Higher Ve Go, Da Deeper Ve Dig"

Dear A to Z:

When you are eighty-two you will look back and smile often. Why? Because you'll be praying, "Thank you, Lord, for the people who have blessed me."

Remember Axel, one of my special blessers? They called him the "Big Swede" because of his native country. And he was one of our nation's prime builders of tall buildings. Tall buildings like the Humble Oil Skyscraper in Houston. Axel was the foreman on that job, and I loved to visit him there.

Often Axel would invite me to attend what he called his "prayer meeting," and I loved it. He would take me up on the stand where he stood above his men; at least one hundred of them. As they looked up to him, he would tell them a story or quote a Scripture verse. I loved it when he said, "You listen now, men. Dis is from da Bible."

Then came his pep talk: "Gentlemen, you are the finest of workmen. You are the greatest of builders. You are the best I have ever assembled." Plus more rah, rah, rah. And you can believe they loved it.

At last, finished, he would say, "Bow your heads. Now ve pray!" Then "Amen," and away they'd go to give him the best they had.

Often the "Big Swede" invited me for what he called "prayer time." Since he invited me often, I got in on every phase of the building. And I will never forget my first visit there.

They were digging the foundation. Down, down, down, and way down. So far down, the human eye could not even begin to see the depth of it.

Of course, the first time I saw it, I exclaimed my awe over and over. To which Axel responded with a statement I've never forgotten. *"Charlie,"* he said, *"Da higher ve go, da deeper ve dig.* You think about that, Charlie. Sometime you preach about that. Ya?"

Ya. Often. And especially when I preach about prayer.

Love, Grandpa

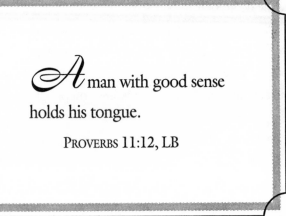

$\mathcal{A}$ man with good sense
holds his tongue.

PROVERBS 11:12, LB

$\mathcal{D}$r. Wilkinson's Advice on How to Pray and When to Keep Silent

———— ∞ ————

Dear A to Z:

My first church out of seminary was in Colorado. Ours was the only church in this little town, and we loved it. Although ministers are not supposed to love one church member more than others, I must confess: I loved Doc Wilkinson with a very special love.

Doc was the only physician for miles around, which meant he was called out often. Midnight. Two A.M. Three-thirty.

So what did that have to do with me? A lot, because I was called out often, too: by the doctor. "Doc" was a firm believer in prayer for all church people, and non-church people, too. He also had an unusual idea about the services of his "Preacher Boy." (Since this was my first church that's what they called me.) The doctor thought his pastor should accompany him on all night calls. He also believed the minister should pray on every call, day or night.

I told Doc I had learned almost nothing at seminary about prayer. So? "So, you go often enough with me, Preacher Boy, and you'll learn." Which I did.

To the sick, to the dying, to the mourning we went. Then,

mission ended, Doc would say in his deep voice, "Bow your heads, folks," and he would nod at me. Could there ever have been a finer school of prayer for any preacher boy?

End of story? No. In our little town there was one "Open All Night" restaurant. Small. Rickety. Right up by the railroad tracks. But a great place for early morning breakfast. And we should know. Every night when we were called out, Doc and I furthered our togetherness here. Pancakes, eggs, bacon, corn bread and "Anything else you guys want?"

The customers in these early hours were fascinating too. Sometimes even members of my congregation were there to greet me. Plus sometimes a bit embarrassed, and rightly so.

On this particular morning I'm sharing with you now, a never-to-be forgotten speech stamped itself forever on my memory. Plus it stamped itself on the memory of some other congregation members too. In small towns like ours, speeches like this get around.

The speaker was a newly elected deacon. His first words when he saw me were, "Oh, no. Not the Preacher Boy. Oh, no."

But, I'll say this for him: He sobered up enough to make his famous address, which I can repeat word for word. Putting an arm around me to brace himself, he held forth for all to hear:

"Preacher Boy. You know how much I think of you. Fact is, whenever your name comes up I give 'em my pep talk. Know what I tell 'em? I tell 'em, 'Anybody talks as much as my Preacher Boy is bound to say something good sooner or later.'"

When the whole restaurant broke up in laughter, Doc leaned over and whispered in my ear, "Keep your mouth shut, Preacher

Boy. Don't say one single word. You hear me?" I heard him, and I didn't say one single word.

As we got in his car when we'd finished breakfast, Doc told me: "Preacher Boy, that crowd in there would have turned anything you said into another big belly laugh. You can't believe what they'll come up with when they're potted. Then the whole town would have two big laughs, one on them, one on you. And some way the biggest one would have been on you. Like the Good Book says, 'There is a time to keep silence.'"

Some day, Dear A to Z, the laughs may be turned on *you*, just as they were on me. I guarantee it will help you to keep humble the rest of your life. Which is a very good thing, even when you're eighty-two.

If it does happen to you, I know you're *smart* enough, dear reader, to remember this story. And *wise* enough to put it in practice. So for a starter let's say it together one more time. Loud. Clear.

There is a time to keep silence.

Love, Grandpa

P.S. The full text of Ecclesiastes 3:7 says: "A time to keep silence, and a time to speak." That's a real nice addition, don't you think?

O come, let us worship and bow down:
let us kneel before the Lord our maker.
PSALMS 95:6, KJV

*W*hy Does God Have Three Names?

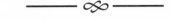

Dear A to Z:

Many times my young friends ask me: "Why do we have three different names for God? I get so mixed up when I try to unravel that in my mind."

I understand how they feel, because during my younger years I was in exactly the same situation. Confused, plus worried for fear I might miss something. But now that I'm older I understand more than I ever did before.

And here's something that helps me.

You have three names, don't you? First name, middle name, last name. Most people go by their first name, but some prefer their middle name. And aren't you glad you have a last name, too? In many places your last name matters most.

Whenever the word "Trinity" surfaces, I pray, "Thank you, Lord, for showing yourself to me in three ways, for giving yourself three names: Father, Son, and Holy Spirit."

Of course, it will take you a lifetime to understand the word "Trinity" enough to satisfy you. But since your lifetime years are sure to pass anyway, why not make it a "thinking" time?

I think God gave us "information sorters" in order for us to know him better; to know other people better; and to know ourselves better.

These information sorters help us to break the big questions into sections, pieces, parts. Each day we can think about one of those pieces. Each day we get to know God a little better.

How many people do you like better the more you get to know them? That's exactly what I hope will happen as you become better acquainted with the Lord. Whenever you hear these two words, "The Lord" (or even the single word "Lord"), say this to yourself:

"The Lord" means Father, Son, and Holy Spirit. These are God's three names. Isn't that nice? He has three names just like I do.'"

But above all, I hope you will give some serious thought and serious study to the name "Jesus." The Bible says he came into our lives to let us know that *GOD IS LOVE.*

Yours for a warm friendship with the Lord,

Love, Grandpa

Church

---∞---

$\mathcal{H}$is mother was ill, so Georgie went to church alone. When he returned he informed his mother that the preacher had preached on "keep your shirt on and you'll get a blanket."

"Now, Georgie, he couldn't have preached on that!" But Georgie insisted that he had. Finally the mother did some checking with the neighbors. They'd been there, too, and this is what the preacher had used as his morning text:

"Be patient, and the Comforter will come."

The Church That Was Founded on Real Horse Sense

———— ∞ ————

Dear A to Z:

We had moved from a fine church in Oklahoma to a non-church in Houston, Texas. Whatever is a non-church? That's when a few people with vision organize a new congregation in a place other than a church building. Here we are on a busy corner. Plenty of room to build, plenty of people to come, let's go folks.

And go we did. We began with an old house in a big pasture, and dreamed of the day we would begin to build there. But until then we'd meet in a junior high school, and have our headquarters at the old house. Lucky, lucky me. I was the first pastor. Good thing, too, because that fit in real well. Our Church Women's Association named our rickety old house "Charlie's Shed."

It was a good thing I knew how to fix broken floors, broken ceilings, broken almost anything. Almost everything in our old house was broken. But we had all kinds of horse sense around including one live horse in a fenced pasture.

Like I said, the house was no beauty, but the *horse* was a top-notcher. A purebred quarter horse. And was he ever an eater. Especially he liked corn, and every day I fed him some corn. Every morning he'd come to my office and stare at me. Whereupon I'd open up the window and feed him a handful or so. (It is not good to over-feed a horse.)

"Solomon's" pedigreed name was something I couldn't even

pronounce. So I called him "Solomon." Very fitting, don't you think? "Solomon" means *wisdom*. And I could tell he was wise by the way he stayed right there when I practiced my sermons.

Always, with breakfast done, he'd stand with his head in the window. Next he would roll his eyes and whinny, which I thought meant, "Continue." So I would give him point one, two, three of this coming Sunday's sermon. At each erudite bit of scholarship he'd whinny again. And I would thank him as I gave him another handful of corn.

Of course, I had my suspicions all along. Could it be that he kept his head in the window because he only wanted more corn? Yes, it could be. That's what his owner thought, too. Nice man, a charter member of our church. But so what if "Solomon" only stayed for another handful of corn? Some kind of wise horse, don't you think?

Now why would I take all this time to tell you about one horse? The reason is this: That church was founded on good solid people sense to go with all that horse sense. Right from the beginning our congregation adopted two basic rules:

1. We began a "Dollar-for-Dollar Program." What did this mean? It meant that every time we spent one dollar on ourselves *we would send one dollar to some mission work where the Lord needed it.* Unbelievable. Unheard of.

And how long did that commitment continue? Well, it's been forty-two years now, and that church is *still a Dollar-for-Dollar Benevolence church.* This year with five thousand members, they have a five million dollar budget. That's two and one-half million for themselves, two and one-half million for missions.

2. Here's the second commitment adopted by this "church of the people sense mixed with horse sense." Every day, every member would be prayed for by some other member. Family by family, that's what they did. Why? *Prayer provides the love to pray for others. Prayer also produces the love to care for what the Bible calls, "The least of these"* (Matthew 25:40).

So thank you, "Solomon." What a beautiful horse you were, in more ways than one. Thank you for hanging out at our rickety old church house. Thank you for staying right there, faithful to whatever your motivation. It was one great start for one great church. Plus it was fun for your admiring preacher.

Love, Grandpa

P.S. Why would I take all this time for such a story? The answer is that you are the hope of tomorrow's church. And I will be praying for you from heaven as you create a wonderful new kind of church. Yes, I'll be praying for you personally, that you will be among the leaders, leading your church in:

1. A prayer-based love for his people here at home.

2. A mission-based commitment for his ministry to others.

$\mathcal{W}$hy Would Father Bill Give a Gift to Presbyterians?

Dear A to Z:

In one town where we lived there was a priest named Bill. Ordinary name, but Bill was no ordinary Catholic priest. Right off we became best friends. He and I met at least weekly for breakfast or lunch. And it was one superior ecclesiastical blending.

As our congregation began to grow, we could see one thing clear and plain. We would soon be needing a new building. Right next to us was the main grocery in our town. Huge. Many, many customers, and they needed a much larger parking lot.

So they made a deal with us. If we'd tear down the old church, the grocery people would buy our site. That would give us a solid financial base to start our new church.

Now comes a story such as I'd never heard before. Nor since. One day, my priest friend Bill arrived with a check for five hundred dollars.

"Charlie," he began, "I am thrilled that you Presbyterians are planning such great things for the future. You know how much I cherish our friendship. So here's one good Catholic's contribution to a good Protestant's chapel."

You can imagine I went into high gear now. "Thank you, thank you, Bill," I said. "What a friend you are. Our people will be thrilled to know you did such a thing. Tell me, isn't this the first time you ever heard of a Catholic priest contributing to the building of a new church for Protestants?"

At this Bill rose, leaned across the desk and with his very best grin he said, "Wait a minute, dear friend. Be sure you get this absolutely clear. My contribution is not for building your new building. *This check is for tearing down your old one.*"

Isn't that one honey of a story? And it really happened. But every time I tell it, some of my Catholic friends will say, "You better be careful where you tell that. Don't you know priests are not supposed to keep money for themselves? Didn't Father Bill know that?"

Yes, Father Bill knew that. But this is what he told me: He came from a wealthy family. Naturally they were proud of Bill. So every now and then they'd give a sizeable gift to their family's favorite priest. And, said he, "Believe me, Charlie, the majority does go to my church. But there is this one little loophole. It is legitimate for me to use a certain percentage as I want to use it.

"Sometimes, you see, I wish to bless those who are not blessed to be Catholics. So here's my check, but don't you forget: This is to help you tear your old church down. Got it?"

Yes, I got it. You can see why my friend Bill and I had so much fun together. Bill was very, very special. And the pope must have thought so too. Soon my friend was honored with the title, "Monsignor." That's a very high honor. My friend Bill deserved to be honored, didn't he?

Love, Grandpa

$\mathcal{W}$henever I go by a church
I stop and pay a visit;
So when they carry me inside
The Lord won't say, "Who is it?"

What Will the Church of Tomorrow Be Like?

——— ∞ ———

Dear A to Z:

What will the church be like when you are eighty-two? Of course, nobody can prophesy absolutely. But you can count on this. The church of tomorrow will be considerably different from the church of today. And better.

So let's have a look:

Whatever happened to the preacher? In so many churches eighty-two years from now, the job of the preacher will be so different. More and more he'll be the pastor, meaning *shepherd*. Won't he preach? Oh, sure, now and then. But not often. Why? Because in the church of tomorrow you might have many, many people who can preach. And it could be the best preaching you ever heard.

But what about the members who don't preach? There are jobs for these people, too. Teachers and counselors, missionaries far away and right here at home, all of them sharing their love with the poor and needy.

You do know also, don't you, that eighty-two years from now our whole social support system will be changed. Why? Because you, dear A to Z, will be saying, "Our Lord said that *we the Church* should care for the poor and needy. Let's lift this burden off the government's shoulders. We should have done that long ago."

Doesn't the Bible say, "Inasmuch as ye have done it unto the least of these, ye have done it unto me"? That, I think, will be your spirit eighty-two years from now. This is what the Lord always wanted: over and over you can read it in the Bible.

Here's another question you'll be asking in the church of tomorrow: "Where have all the denominations gone?" Whatever happened to all those many labels? Oh, they were dropped back down the road somewhere.

Does this mean the new church will have fewer people worshipping? Oh, no, no, no. Instead, it means many, many more attending services and working to serve the Lord. Why? Could it be that this church of our distant tomorrow is more what the Lord always wanted?

Yes, that could be.

When will these things happen? Like the Bible says, nobody can prophesy all things for sure. But if you are a caring believer, I believe you'll be saying:

"Hurrah for the church of tomorrow!"

And who's going to bring forth the new church, with the name of Christ in its forehead?

Go look in the mirror. *You are.*

Love, Grandpa

God's Littlest Angel and His Pearl of Truth

Dear A to Z:

Here is a beautiful legend I know you'll like. It's about creation's very earliest days. God had finished the universe, and now he had only one thing left to do. He must create concepts and ideas necessary for the good life.

That would be a big job, wouldn't it? But God didn't mind big jobs. So he worked hard putting all his thoughts together. "Ah," he said, "we will name this last one, 'The Pearl of Truth.'"

Then finished, he called one of his favorite angels, the littlest angel, to deliver "Truth." Tender story? Yes. But alas and alack, the littlest angel stumbled over a star and fell with The Pearl of Truth. And you know what happened.

The Pearl of Truth fell to earth and shattered into millions of pieces.

Could this be why pure truth is so hard to find sometimes? Yes, it could. Doesn't this also mean there are many bits of truth yet to be discovered? Many people, finding even one small piece of truth exclaim, "Look, I have found Truth." (But we won't have it all ... until we get to heaven.)

What does this story say to you and to me about our attitudes toward other people who see "Truth" differently than we see it? What about different teachings, different beliefs, different cultures?

And yet, remember also the parable of Jesus:

> The kingdom of heaven is like a merchant in search of fine pearls, who, on finding one pearl of great value, went and sold all that he had and bought it.
>
> MATTHEW 13:45-46, RSV

How are you doing on your pearl hunt? Makes us think, doesn't it?

Love, Grandpa

— ∞ —

Jesus said ... "I am the way, the truth, and the life."
JOHN 14:6

— ∞ —

Heaven

*M*y times are in thy hand.

PSALMS 31:15

$\mathcal{W}$hen We Get to Heaven Will We Know Each Other?

Dear A to Z:

A dear friend of mine once asked me an important question:"I had a baby sister, but she only lived a few weeks. Do you think she and I will know each other when I get to heaven?"

"Will we know each other?" How many times have I heard that question? Many, many times. Mothers grieving the loss of a child; men who have just buried their wives; wives mourning their husbands; grandparents, all asking the same basic question.

Martha had a little sister who lived only a few days. Martha often wondered if her sister would still be a baby in heaven. She and her mother loved to discuss that question often.

Timothy, our youngest son, was especially close to his grandmother, and he had a fascinating idea. One day when he was still in grade school, he was visiting with his grandmother when he said to her, "I think, Grandma, your baby girl will be whatever you want her to be. Sometimes she will be a baby. Sometimes she will be grown up if you want her grown up."

How would he know? The truth is, nobody knows for sure. But doesn't the Bible say, "a little child shall lead them"?

Philippians 3:20-21 gives us a fascinating bit of light:

But our commonwealth [citizenship] is in heaven,
and from it we await a Savior, the Lord Jesus Christ,
who will change our lowly body to be like his glorious body...

PHILIPPIANS 3:20-21, RSV

Did you hear that?

*Our bodies in heaven will be like the body of Jesus after his resur-
rection!*

All right. Praise the Lord. That must mean we'll know each
other, won't we? The disciples knew Jesus after the Resurrection,
and Mary recognized him, too.

Look it up. You'll love it. A concordance (a wonderful book
containing Scripture "guide word"s) will help you to find what
you'd like to know. Get a friend, too, to study this fascinating
question with you. Do what the Bible calls, "searching the
Scriptures." On this theme you'll thrill to what you find.

So why won't I tell you exactly where you could look in the
Bible? I don't want to destroy your fun. That word "fun" is the
right word. You give God's Word a solid try and you, too, will
say, "Amen. The Bible really *is* fun."

Love, Grandpa

*N*o Marriages in Heaven?

———— ∞ ————

Dear A to Z:

Often, very often, people ask me, "Do you really think it's true there'll be no marriages in heaven?" It's a frequent question, even among the young. Especially if they're falling in love. "You mean, no marriages in heaven?" they ask. "Doesn't seem fair, does it?"*

But why should we be bothering our psyches over such an item? In his Book God tells us, "Eye hath not seen, nor ear heard, neither have entered into the heart of man, the things which God hath prepared for them that love him" (1 Corinthians 2:9).

Martha and I clung to that verse. Especially when we knew it wouldn't be long for her, we'd repeat it together. And at the end, we'd say, "Thank you, heavenly Father. We're counting on that verse. If you have something better than marriage for us in heaven, here's a big 'thank you' from us."

Love, Grandpa

*If you would like to study this further, read Mark 12:24-25;Luke 20:34-35.

"Oh, I See"

——— ∞ ———

Dear A to Z:

Some things are almost impossible to understand, aren't they?

A nice grandma gets cancer. Your friend is paralyzed in an automobile accident. Your neighbor's house burned to the ground. Your teacher's baby didn't live. Why? Why? Why?

How can we believe in a loving God in the face of downers like these? Nice people hurt. Good people cry. Terrible things happen. Everywhere. And like the Bible says, "He sendeth rain on the just and the unjust." Good things do sometimes happen to people who lie and cheat and steal. That's not fair either.

Is there any way to explain these things? Is there any light strong enough to penetrate these awful awfuls?

You can believe that even a minister doesn't know all the answers. But here is the thought that has helped me when I stand by a grave and cry with people. Where the thought came from I do not know. But I do know this beautiful thought sounds in my heart again and again:

Someone once said, "The first thing we'll say when we get to heaven is 'Oh, I see.'"

Three great words: "Oh, I see."

Love, Grandpa

*T*each us to number our days aright that we may gain a heart of wisdom.

PSALMS 90:12, NIV

$\mathscr{A}$ Lesson from Annie Lou

Dear A to Z:

Your grandmother and I were riding the train to a Midwestern speaking engagement. We flew so much, if there was time we enjoyed train rides. And we wouldn't have missed this one for anything.

This was the day we met Annie Lou. She couldn't have been more than four or five because she wasn't in school yet. Her charming, bright eyes sparkled with the fun of living.

She had been running up and down the aisles for some time now. Then she decided it was time to settle down and, lucky us, she cuddled up beside us to visit.

Since we had not seen anyone with her on her aisle runs, we were curious.

"Annie Lou, where are you going?"

"I don't know." This with a shrug of her shoulders.

"Oh, but you must know what town you're going to?"

"No." Absolutely not. Destination unknown.

Worried, we asked, "But, Annie Lou, isn't someone coming to meet you at the station?"

"I don't know."

"This doesn't seem right, Annie Lou, if you don't know where you're going, how will you know where to get off when you get there?"

On and on and on two panicky adults grilled the little girl. We grew increasingly alarmed with each unanswered question.

Finally, when she could stand it no longer, Annie Lou got up. With pure, little-girl disgust, she put hands on hips and announced, "I don't need to know all those things. See? I'm traveling with my father, and he knows all those things."

Beautiful lesson, never forgotten. A lesson we needed then. A lesson we'll always need.

I don't need to worry. You don't need to worry. This trip we're on is with our Father.

Love, Grandpa

*S*urely you know that you are God's temple and that God's spirit lives in you!

1 CORINTHIANS 3:16,
TODAY'S ENGLISH VERSION

Epilogue

Three Sure Tests of Maturity

Dear A to Z:

Read the Bible verse on the opposite page again. That's you. That's "What You Is." You are a dwelling place for God's Spirit to live in you. He wants to guide you, to teach you, to use you. And that's awesome, isn't it?

In this last of our letters we will think together about
"Maturity."
The dictionary says that "maturity" means:

"Full development—being completed."

So if God made you, if he has a plan for you, then this is life's all-time goal for you. To be fully developed, complete in his plan.

In this last letter I invite you to think with me on three questions. Three questions to help you be what God meant you to be.

Question One: *Am I increasingly able to pray, "Lord, think through me. Help me to care more for what you think, rather than taking my cues from the crowd"?*

Maturity in the Lord is the ability to stand up against the squeeze. You know the familiar lines, "Everybody's doing it." "You've got to go along to be popular." "Don't be a square."

The world is overloaded with chameleon-like people who take their color from the background. Brown with the brown, green with the green, colorless with the colorless.

Think for a minute how Jesus must have felt when he was up for trial. The Bible says, "He was tempted like as we are." That means this line might have occurred to him: "Give me a moment, sir. I'm sure I can make a statement satisfactory to all concerned."

Ever the winds of popular opinion blow, and how they affect us depends on us. Are you the weather-vane type, merely showing which way the wind is blowing? Or do you stand fast, helping to determine which way the wind will blow?

So this is one of the sure tests for both *smart* and *wise* thinking. More and more can you pray and mean it, "Lord, think through me."

Question Two: *Am I increasingly able to analyze what's wrong with me, rather than projecting the blame on others?*

A telescope is a great instrument because it helps us see far ahead. That's good for planning and thinking about tomorrow and the years off there in our future.

A microscope is a great instrument too. It helps us see things unbelievable to the naked eye. Very important at times.

But if you could only take one instrument down life's road, what would it be? How about a *mirror?* And why? I like this poem for an answer:

An enemy I had whose mien I stoutly strove to know;
For hard he dogged my steps unseen wherever I might go.
At last I seized and held him fast, the veil from him did draw
I looked into his beady eyes and lo, myself I saw.

Author unknown, but thank you poet, I needed that. And you'll need it, too, dear A to Z. Especially when you're still young, you'll need it. Why? Because in your early years, adults are stupid. Father is stupid, mother is stupid, and teachers, are they ever stupid!

But now comes the day. You're growing up when you can pray: "Lord, take me down the hall to a mirror. Am I looking more and more like you want me to look?"

Question Three: *Am I increasingly able to focus on what I can do for the Lord, rather than what I can do for me?*

This has to be the acid test for being what God made us to be. And oh, the influences to get us thinking otherwise.

Turn on your radio. Dial the tube. Flip the pages of that magazine. Read the newspaper ads. What do you get?

"Be nice to yourself...." "You deserve the best...." "Give yourself a treat...." "Drive our sports car...." "You owe it to your family...." "Drink our drink. It's good for jittery nerves. And if you don't have jittery nerves, it's good for that too."

Thus the gimmee-guys shout their wares, and before we know it, they've got us hooked.

Or are you getting too *wise* for their blather? Honestly can you say in your heart, "No way, pal. I was put here by the Lord to be more of a giver than a grabber."

It's time to say goodbye. Thank you for thinking with me about who you are and why you're here. I do believe you are the *smartest* generation that ever came to live here. And I do pray that you will be *wise* enough to let God have his way with you.

Sometimes at night when my room is dark, when I am about to drift away, a picture comes across my screen of thought.

It is the picture of a wonderful new world, with wonderful new people, with wonderful new ideas. And you are the new people, my grandchildren. You and your friends. Your generation. But see over there. There stands God with a lantern in his hand and he is saying:

**"Surely, thou art come to the kingdom
for such a time as this."**

That, I think, is the Lord's call to you and me.

Love, Grandpa

P.S. How long will it take you to become fully mature in the Lord? If you're like I am, it will be sometime after eighty-two.

Other Books of Interest by Charlie Shedd

Letters to Karen and Letters to Philip: Two-in-One Gift Edition. Time-tested Christian advice for young couples on how to make love last a lifetime.
$17.99 hardcover

How to Make People Really Feel Loved (and Other Life-Giving Observations). Secrets for strengthening relationships with families and friends, and for rising to life's great challenges.
$12.99 hardcover

Brush of an Angel's Wing. Inspiring tales of God's unseen messengers who help us, protect us, and guide us.
$14.99 hardcover, $10.99 paperback

What Children Tell Me About Angels. This beautiful volume includes stories of "unseen angel" blessings, told through the eyes of children.
$12.99 hardcover

Available at your local Christian bookstore, or send check or money order to Servant Publications, P.O. Box 8617, Ann Arbor, MI 48107. For each book ordered please include $3.25 postage and handling.

If you would like information about other books by Charlie Shedd such as *How Can We Know if We're Really in Love*, write to the following address and request a price list:

Charlie's Books
700 Whit Davis Road
Athens, GA 30605